# The
# Golf
## Instructor

# The
# Golf
## Instructor

*An illustrated guide
from tee to green*

## Michael Hobbs

CHARTWELL
BOOKS, INC.

A QUANTUM BOOK

Published by Chartwell Books
A Division of Book Sales Inc.
114 Northfield Avenue
Edison, New Jersey 08837
USA

ISBN 0-7858-1561-9

QUMFTTG

This book is produced by
Quantum Publishing Ltd.
6 Blundell Street
London N7 9BH

Printed in Singapore by Star Standard Industries (Pte) Ltd

The material in this book previously appeared in

*Golf Instructor's Library: Off the Tee*
*Golf Instructor's Library: From the Fairway*
*Golf Instructor's Library: On the Green*
*Golf Instructor's Library: Troubleshooting*

# CONTENTS

# PREFACE

I am a left-handed golfer. However, over the years I haven't found it difficult to follow golf instruction writing, which is traditionally directed at right-handers.

As a golf writer, I know that always mentioning each form of the golfing species is easily possible, but leads to many repetitive phrases that impair the readability of the book. As a left-hander I know we have learned to cope in a 90 per cent right-handed world. A right-hander, on the other hand, is far less able. I don't think he could follow a text written for left-handers – imagine him trying to use left-handed scissors or knock in a tack, grasping the hammer left-handed. What injuries and incompetence would result for this less adaptable and accomplished sector of the human species!

# ACKNOWLEDGEMENTS

Above all, I should like to thank Grenville Warne for being a splendid model for my instructional photography. He gave up many hours throughout a whole season when he would surely far rather have been playing than demonstrating. His help has been invaluable.

I should like to thank my main golf club, Tracy Park near Bristol, England, for allowing me to carry out most of the instruction photography on its splendid 27 holes. I also thank other clubs for more limited photographic facilities.

The club's professional, Grant Aitken, and his son and assistant professional Kelvin, have also been invariably helpful with advice, information and allowing me to use equipment for illustrations.

At Quintet Publishing, I should particularly like to thank David Barraclough for his continuous work throughout the project and also Peter Arnold who was responsible for the detailed copy editing. My thanks are also due to Rob Shone for his production of drawings and diagrams and the design team at Bridgewater Design.

Michael Hobbs                                    Worcester, England

# HOLDING THE CLUB FOR FULL SHOTS

Even champions have used unconventional, and for that matter, downright bad grips. One can remember Gene Sarazen in the past, and Lee Trevino, now a dominant force on the US Seniors Tour. Among today's top tournament professionals, the same could be said for Paul Azinger and Bernhard Langer, and among the ladies, there's Nancy Lopez, all of whom place their left hands in a position which many would consider wrong.

They're all outstanding golfers, so one is entitled to ask if they're right and the rest of the golfing world at fault. The answer is that, if you are to use an unconventional grip, then compensations must be made elsewhere in the swing. A relatively poor player may well find that this doesn't work at all, while a more talented golfer will experience periods of poor play.

So there are very good arguments for using a conventional grip. We now need to define just what that is. It might be useful if you have a club to hand while we're doing this.

The first thing to remember is that the club is held mainly in the fingers – and small variations will apply depending on whether you have long and lean, or more spatulate ones. Start with the idea that the basic grip is palm-to-palm, with the handle of the club in between. Now let's take one hand at a time, first noting where the club lies across the open hand.

The handle should run from the bottom joint of the little finger of the left hand to the first joint of the forefinger, and you'll note that the palm is a definite help at the little finger end. The right-hand grip lies just a little more in the fingers themselves, perhaps by no more than a quarter of an inch.

Ready to play.

How the club lies across the left hand.

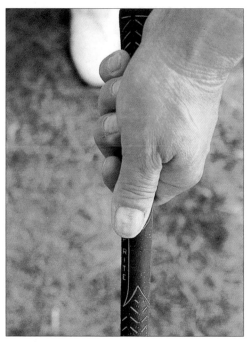

Left hand closed.

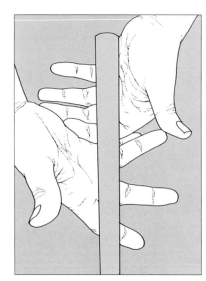

How the club lies across the open hands.

Now, allow your hand to close naturally, and note the position of your thumbs. You'll find that they lie almost straight down the shaft, with the left thumb offset a little to the right, and the right thumb to the left. Looking down from your stance position, you should see only the first two knuckles of your left hand.

This is the basic, conventional grip; all fingers on the shaft, with the hands nestling close together. However, because the hands tend to work better in unison if they are more definitely linked, this grip is seldom taught today.

## THE 'VARDON' GRIP

Early golf clubs featured much thicker grips than today's implements. This meant that most good players nestled the club much more firmly in the palms than you'll see around the circuits today: neither thumb rested on the shaft.

Over the years, shafts became thinner and, round about 1890, a few people began to use a new way of melding the hands together. The right hand moved a little way up the shaft with the little finger no longer gripping it. Instead, it came to rest over the left forefinger, or perhaps a little further up, in the gap between the first two fingers.

How the club lies across the right hand.

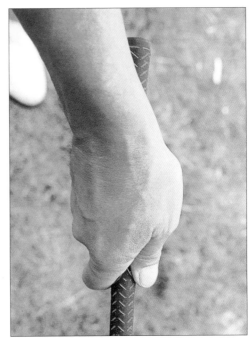

Right hand closed.

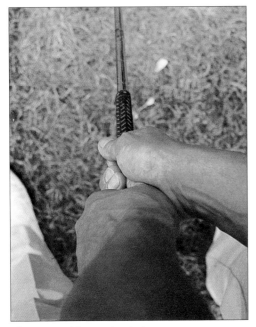

Player's view of the completed grip.

The double overlapping grip – a variation on the Vardon grip.

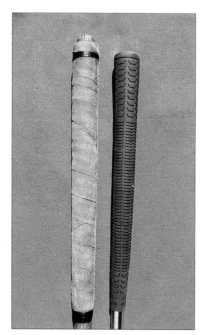

A thicker sheepskin grip of the past and a modern rubber grip.

The interlocking grip.

The rest of the golfing world was slow to follow suit, because most of the best players carried on in the same old way. However, from the mid-1890's, the 'Great Triumvirate' of J H Taylor, Harry Vardon and James Braid all adopted the 'overlap' grip, and people began to sit up and take notice. Obviously, if the 'Great Triumvirate' did it, it must be right.

Quite naturally, special attention was paid to Harry Vardon, who between 1896 and 1900 played a quality of golf that had never been seen before. Not only that, but he *looked* the perfect golfer as well, and his grip was much imitated. Eventually it became called the 'Vardon Grip'. Not that he, in fact, invented it, or was particularly unusual in using it.

## THE INTERLOCKING GRIP

This, again, is simply a way to link the hands together. Here, the left forefinger isn't on the shaft at all. It rests in the gap

The Great Triumvirate – Taylor, Braid and Vardon – by Clement Flower, 1913.

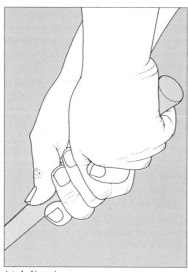

Interlocking grip.

A double overlapping grip on the green.

between the last two fingers of the right hand, with the right little finger placed between forefinger and middle finger of the left hand.

If you use this grip, you'll notice that only three fingers of each hand (plus the thumbs, as before), rêst on the club shaft. For many, this grip doesn't feel comfortable, but it is an effective way of locking the hands together. Most professionals prefer the Vardon Grip, but Jack Nicklaus and Greg Norman use the interlock, so it must have much to recommend it.

## VARIATIONS

Just as the ten-fingered grip is out of favor, quite a few excellent players have adopted more overlap than is the norm. It's quite possible to overlap two fingers, and some players have even extended this to three, which leaves only the forefinger on the actual grip of the club. Usually, this is

Where the Vs should point.

Hands turned anti-clockwise.

The Vs have dropped below the right shoulder.

done by players who want to minimize the domination of their right hands, often to avoid hooking

# CHECKING ON WHERE THE 'V's POINT

The gaps between forefinger and thumb of both right and left hands form a 'V' shape when the hands close around the club. When you view this from your stance, or in a mirror, the apex of both V's should point approximately towards your right shoulder.

There are variations, however. Professionals with particularly strong and lively hands have often turned both of them a little counter-clockwise. Those V's will then point somewhere between the chin and the point of the right shoulder, depending on what they feel works best for them. But please note – no one goes in the other direction, so that the V's drop to below the right shoulder.

# RULES AND COURSE BEHAVIOR

Far too many golfers, when they first take up the game, get their priorities wrong.

First, probably, comes the appealing glitter and sheen of a brand new set of clubs. It might be closely matched by color coordinated clothing, with matching umbrella and golfbag. Amazingly, this often happens before the golfer has taken a single lesson, even before he or she has tried hitting a single golf ball. Remember, though most have sufficient innate ability to become reasonable players eventually, there is, alas, a small minority who don't.

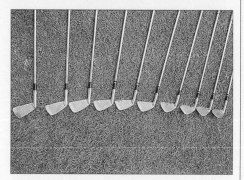

A full set of irons clearly showing the varying degrees of loft.

Before going to all this expense, I advise you go to a practice range and, perhaps even more important, have a few lessons. This will ensure you start correctly as regards, for example, the right grip and stance. Some things, these in particular, are very hard to change once they become ingrained.

Even if you pass these hurdles successfully, you are still not ready to step on to a golf course.

Why? Well, have you thought of acquainting yourself with the rules of golf and behavior on the course? The rules are lengthy and sometimes difficult to understand. They have to be complicated because the game is played cross country. You can find yourself in situations that could not possibly occur in the strictly defined areas used in tennis, football and squash, for example. There is probably no other game that is so complex as regards the rules, and all as a result of the terrain over which the game is played.

It isn't the aim of *The Golf Instructor* to set out all the rules of golf. That would take a book in itself to both explain the rules and give examples of their application. However, all is by no means lost. Books are already available on the subject and both the Royal and Ancient Golf Club of St Andrews and the United States Golf Association provide rule books of a size which can be kept permanently in your golf bag.

Golf course behavior is a little different. You will easily find short passages on 'etiquette', but these don't go into sufficient detail. Even if you attempt to study the subject, there will still be gaps in your knowledge which can only be filled by watching how experienced players conduct themselves during a round of golf.

But what is at the root of 'etiquette'? The word makes it sound rather like a Victorian manual aimed at teaching people how to handle the cutlery at upper class dinner parties or how to address the wife of the president of the United States or the consort of the Queen of England!

Golfing 'etiquette' is how you behave towards both your fellow golfers and the golf course.

For this book I'll confine myself to how you behave on the tee as a player in the most common form of golf, a fourball.

Firstly, it is obviously quite important to avoid killing or maiming your companions! Be very careful about those loosening up practice swings. Drift a reasonable distance away from your fellow players. A golf club is a lethal weapon. A clubhead travelling at around 100 mph can crack a skull, blind a person and break all manner of bones. Make sure no one is anywhere near where you are swinging your club and remember that your fellow players may easily wander into the path of your swing.

Also remember that – even if only occasionally – clubheads have been known to fly off. Make the aim of your swing, therefore, in the opposite direction to where your fellow golfers are standing.

Quite often in those swings, you'll be taking divots. Your fellow players will not wish to be hit by flying turf. You may feel that this is unlikely to do much bodily harm, but being hit in the face, or simply having divots flying close by, can be quite a shock. And you could dislodge a stone along with the turf divot and remove someone's eye. Once more, then, direct your swing away from other golfers.

The next danger to other players comes when you stand on the tee and play your shot. You are unlikely to be wild enough to strike a member of your fourball this time, but beware of others on the golf course. Are you quite sure that the players in the match immediately ahead of you are out of range? Imagine that you are going to hit the longest drive of your life. If you are confident that you won't reach anyone playing ahead, play your shot, but bear in mind that we only know our length limits on very familiar courses. Very few have good enough judgement to know that, say, 270 yards is the distance to the third oak tree along the right-hand side of the fairway  Caution is therefore the watch word and you'll only need to wait a few seconds for those ahead to walk the extra yards.

These players are not out of range.

There are other players on the course and you need to glance around. Perhaps there's a tee with a group of players standing on it within range. A glance at your scorecard, or even a notice on your own tee, may tell you that you are not permitted to drive off when that other tee is occupied.

Golf courses also frequently have parallel fairways. Is there someone ahead who has come into your line of fire in order to play their ball? If so, you have 'right of way' but you may feel guilty if your ball strikes this player.

There may be other players within range but, because most golf courses are busy, no one can be expected to wait until there is no possibility of your ball hitting players should you happen to be very wild.

However, there's still something you are required to do in these circumstances. Be ready to give a full-throated cry of 'Fore!'

But perhaps you shouldn't be on the tee at all. Is it actually your turn to play? If you are a beginner, or a stranger at the particular golf club, follow their procedures. In a strokeplay competition, for instance, it's usual for the order on the draw sheet to be followed. In fourball play, it may be the club tradition that the golfer with the lowest handicap is the first to tee off. Most often it is done 'by lot' – in other words the toss of a coin. In all this, there isn't really a problem. Just have the courtesy to ask or wait until others tell you.

The players watching this tee shot are in correct positions.

Now let's turn to the behavior expected of you when another member of your game is on the tee. It's quite simple and mainly concerns where you stand and what not to do. You shouldn't stand behind the player's line of shot since many object to this, nor should you stand too far in front. Both these positions can catch your fellow golfer's eye and are distracting. Similarly you should not be behind the player's back. Golfers about to hit the ball are very often nervy fellows. They like to know where you are. Therefore, you stand, not too close, facing their chest and, of course, clear of the teeing ground.

Well, we've now got you in the right place. You are still in a position where any movement could catch his or her eye. So stand still and don't make any noise. You shouldn't, for example, be talking to other players, causing coins to chink in your pocket or moving your golf bag.

As with all rules of golf or golf behavior, there are exceptions. When the light is dim near dusk,

The player on the right is too far behind the driver.

or if a low sun is shining into a player's eyes, it is difficult to follow the flight of the ball. In such cases, it's certainly permissible to stand behind the player's line of shot. You are far more likely to be able to track the ball from that position rather than side on. But ask first.

It's also a courtesy to follow the flight of your fellow players' golf balls. You hope they'll do the same for you. It also saves time. The striker, even in the clearest of light, may fail to catch sight of their ball, usually if it's flown high or to right or left.

Also make a mental note of where other golf balls finish. It can prevent a long search and, of course, a lost ball that would have easily been found if, in this case, four golfers were looking in the right area.

Nowadays much time is devoted to golf on television. Usually this shows golfers playing for

their livelihood and often large amounts of money. One result is many tournament players take the game at a very slow pace. They debate their choice of club, select one and then have a change of mind. Quite often more than once. When the decision is eventually made, a few practice swings may follow and the golfer takes some time examining their target line from behind the ball. Then a stance is taken up and a few, or perhaps a large number of waggles follow. All that done, and there may still be a pause before taking the momentous decision to begin the backswing.

Keep in mind how relatively quickly golf used to be played before we began to imitate the stars. Indeed, the stars of bygone days also played at a fast pace. The golfer used to walk quickly, make up their mind on choice of club and how to play it before reaching their ball, and then took up their stance briskly and swung. Two hours for a two ball to play 18 holes was the norm, and not so very much more for four players.

Alas, that's not remotely possible today, except when you have the luck to find an empty course ahead of you. If you are a paragon of briskness, you will still be held up by the players in your own game and blocked by the games ahead of you.

The best you can aim for is not to be the cause of slow play. Always bear in mind how golfers of the past approached the game.

All this has to do with behavior, rather than that word 'etiquette' in its old-fashioned sense. However, the word does come into the modern game of golf as regards clothing.

It is correct to stand behind a player when the light is dim.

Time to consider packing up and returning to the clubhouse. Playing in the dark can be dangerous.

The part of the teeing area you are concerned with is a rectangle. It is the area defined by an imaginary straight line drawn between the tee markers you are playing from that day, extending towards the rear of the teeing ground for two club (driver) lengths, with a second parallel line drawn across to complete the rectangle. You must not place your ball any nearer to the hole than the front line, or anywhere else outside the dimensions of the rectangle. If you do, you are penalized two strokes in strokeplay (and disqualified if you don't replay the shot) and can be required to replay the tee shot in matchplay. Most opponents will only

Many golfers like to get themselves up in resplendent garb. If you are one, I have no objections. I'll simply concentrate on a few of the 'don'ts'.

Dress rules at golf clubs vary and have a broad range. At your own club, you simply have to learn them and conform. If they are, some might say, too lax, this won't necessarily be the case elsewhere.

You are never wrong, however, kitted out in a pair of golf shoes, slacks, a shirt with a collar and a plain sweater. That's simple enough. However, if you turn out in, for example, trainers, shorts or jeans, a tee shirt and a jockey cap you could easily not be allowed on the course.

The point to bear in mind is that, all over the world, clubs and public courses are not at all strict about golf clothing – but there are restrictions from time to time and it's easy to avoid offending.

So much for behavior. Though the rules of golf are generally complex, they aren't as regards tee shots since you are on the only part of a golf course that is defined as exactly as the dimensions of, for example, a tennis court.

This ball is clearly not in front of the tee marker.

**TOP AND ABOVE:** Look for a good flat tie on the tee, rather than tee up as far as possible.

ask you to do this if you hit a particularly good shot. The penalty is far less severe than in strokeplay, but certainly irritating if you've just dispatched a screamer of a drive or holed in one at a par 3.

A surprising number of people do tee their ball up just an inch or two further forward than the rules allow, even though the advantage is virtually non-existant. Is a drive of 260 yards 3 inches really any better than one of 260 yards. The extra distance might mean your ball just reaches a bunker or divot hole. Remember, your fellow golfers in matchplay will seldom require you to replay the shot. But they will almost always notice and put you down in their memories as a cheat. In strokeplay, they are required to take action.

However, there is no reason why you shouldn't take maximum advantage of the rectangle. Examine it for a flat lie or perhaps just the merest suggestion of an upslope, if that's what you prefer. Be prepared to lose a little distance to get this. Also make sure that you have chosen ground which provides a good stance, so that you won't, for instance, have a foot on a loose divot.

In order to hit away from trouble along the left, tee up on the extreme left of the tee.

Incidentally, only the ball has to be within the teeing rectangle – you don't. Though it is rarely an advantage to stand outside, there are occasions when it can be. These are frequently ignored by the vast majority of golfers. Let's suppose there's a frightening hazard all along the left of the fairway ahead. You want to aim away from it. The further left you stand, the better. So why not take full advantage of the rules and stand outside the teeing area?

Having now made all the decisions, you are ready to play your shot and the ball falls off the tee peg. You can simply replace it, without penalty. But this time be sure it's secure on its perch. If it falls off as your clubhead approaches the ball, even a reasonable shot is unlikely and the stroke counts if you are in the process of making it.

Now, you've hit your ball away and, alas, it's heading for wild country where you are not confident that you can find the ball. After the remaining players have teed off, you have the option of playing another shot. But first you have a decision to make. You can declare the ball lost, in which case it's officially abandoned. You can't play it even if it is later found. You have penalized yourself one stroke and distance, and your second tee shot counts as your third.

Often, however, golfers simply don't know whether or not they are going to find a ball. In this case, tell your fellow golfers that you are playing a 'provisional ball'. There is nothing in the rules to prevent your doing so after every shot and you certainly should whenever you are unsure whether your ball will be found.

In this instance, if your first tee shot is found, you must play that ball. Should it be in an unplayable lie, you should follow the rules for that situation (dealt with in *Trouble Shooting*).

Playing one (even two) provisional balls is often sensible. If your first shot is lost, it avoids the delay of having to walk back to the tee.

Just as there are simple dress pointers to follow before you play off the first tee, so you must be equipped as the rules of golf require. Remember to check that you have no more than 14 clubs in your bag. If you find an extra one, you don't have to dispose of it. You can nominate to your fellow players which club is out of play.

Each club must also conform to the rules of the game, but there should be no problem with manufactured clubs. Should you happen to make yourself a club, however, look up the rules regarding what constitutes an illegal piece of equipment.

As regards your ball, you should make sure you can identify it. Strictly speaking, just to know you are playing, say, a number 4 Titleist isn't quite good enough. For a start, declare the make and number of your ball to your fellow players to avoid any confusion. To make doubly sure, put an identifying mark on your ball.

# STANDING AND SWINGING

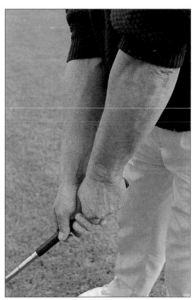

A tight Vardon grip.

Professionals, who play and practice every day, develop extremely strong hands. It doesn't take them any special effort to hold the club very firmly indeed when playing a full swing. In contrast, club golfers play very much less, often averaging, say, one game per weekend, so obviously, their fingers don't have the opportunity to become nearly as strong as those of a professional.

Nevertheless, it's important to avoid gripping the club tightly, forcing the muscles of forearm, upper arm and shoulders to become taut.

Unfortunately, it *feels* necessary to grip tightly, because everyone is aware how important the hands are: they are, after all, the only connection between the club and you. The answer is to concentrate on being firm, not tight. It's impossible to swing back and through freely with a tight grip, and it's all too easy to lose vital clubhead speed.

Keep supple on the backswing. Your grip will firm up quite naturally when in the hitting area.

Reaching for the ball.

A cramped stance.

## FINDING YOUR NATURAL BALL POSITION

Many poor golfers stand with the ball too far away, and therefore find themselves leaning over much too far when attempting to make a full shot. Far fewer people stand too close to the ball, inhibiting their ability to swing freely. Somewhere between these two extremes there's a right position for you. Here's how to find it.

Stand with your feet apart, at about shoulder width. Stand erect, with knees flexed, bottom slightly out, and let your arms support the club, not allowing it to dangle. Now, without bending your back, lean down from the waist. The spot where the clubhead touches the ground is where your ball should be.

Feet at shoulder width.

Now bend from the waist.

And you're in the right position.

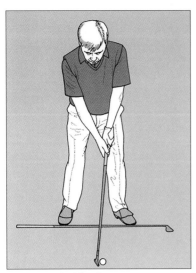

Using a club to check feet alignment.

**ABOVE AND OPPOSITE:** This par 4 is occasionally driveable – wind behind, running fairway – but usually it would be better to play an accurate iron shot. There's a tree in play close by on the left, bunkers beyond, and on the right, more trees.

## THE FEET

Observe your feet when you're walking normally. Henry Cotton is slightly pigeon toed, and stood to the ball that way. Most of us, however, splay our toes outward to some degree, and you should do the same when standing to the ball.

A line drawn across your toes should be exactly parallel with a line from your ball to the target.

At some point, you might like to experiment with your left foot drawn back, just a little, but begin from the normal position – and remember, shoulders and hips must also be parallel with the target line.

**Visualizing the line to the target.**

## AIM THE CLUBFACE

Far too many golfers think of settling into position over the ball. There is, then, much shuffling of feet to line up for the shot, and concentration on having the ball a comfortable distance away. Only after that do they look up to see where the target is.

*Wrong!*

There's a much better way of going about things. As you walk up to the ball, visualize a line from it to the target. When you arrive, first aim your club face along that target line. It's up to you how you do it.

Most golfers used to do this with just the left hand on the club, and then add the other hand once they were satisfied that the clubface was on line. Today, right-hand-first is more popular.

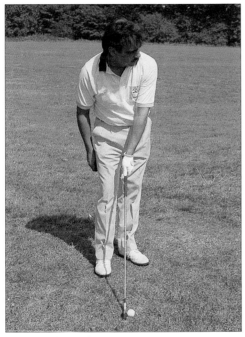

Aligning the left hand first.

Aligning right hand first.

**ABOVE LEFT AND RIGHT:** The player is reaching round, not under, to get his right hand in position.

25

**ABOVE LEFT AND RIGHT:** Here, he reaches under. Note how the right shoulder is lower than the left now.

This does give one very clear advantage. Many poor players tend to reach *round* to place the right hand in position when the left hand is placed on the club first. But, if you are going to keep your shoulders square with the target line, you must reach *under* with your right hand. Reaching round throws the shoulders, and very possibly the hips as well, wide open. A slice or pull hook is the virtually certain result.

Once you have your hands on the club, and the face is aimed, let the rest of your body join in. This means aligning the shoulder and hips along the target line, getting the distance between you and the ball right, and allowing the knees to flex slightly.

This is the orthodox square position. After much experiment, however, many good players have found that it suits them better to stand in a slightly open position, left foot withdrawn from the line by an inch or two. They maintain that this helps them not to hook the ball, and that it allows them to swing through more freely because the left hip is not so much 'in the way'.

But the converse isn't true. If you are a slicer, you won't find a cure by moving your left foot a little closer to the ball. For most people, the increased difficulty of swinging freely through and clearing your hips will make cutting across the ball more likely.

Some like to set the right foot in position first.

Seve Ballesteros demonstrates his driving technique.

# SWINGING BACK

The most important part of the backswing is unarguably the very first movement, simply because it influences everything that follows. Those first two or three inches can make or destroy a swing.

Some players need a trigger to start the whole thing off, a movement of some kind *towards* the ball. This is just an aid to starting the take-away, so there's nothing rigid about it; it can be made with knees, hands or legs and is almost imperceptible.

Many players also find a preliminary 'waggle' is useful. This is a rehearsal, in miniature, of the whole swing. The golfer moves the clubhead a foot or two away from the ball, then brings it back to what will be the point of impact.

This shouldn't be a vague waving of the club to and fro. The idea isn't merely to loosen the muscles and relax the nerves, but rather to programme the muscles for the task ahead.

The 'waggle' will differ from shot to shot. It will be very different for a full drive than for a little high lob shot over a bunker with the green close behind. In the first case you will be rehearsing power; in the second, a delicate touch.

Some players take a rather different view of the 'waggle' They are interested in just the very beginning of the take-away, the part which gets the whole swing going rhythmically and in line. They are reassuring themselves and programming the muscle memory for the beginning of the take-away.

Yet many play with no apparent movements of any kind, once they have settled into the stance. My own opinion is that there are, in fact, such movements but they are internal and imperceptible. The golfer is, perhaps, feeling his or her balance and making minute changes to weight distribution – a little, more or less, towards the heels. Often that motionless period can be quite brief, in the case of a player like Seve Ballesteros. It may be the result of the player waiting until he or she 'feels ready'.

This waggle rehearses the beginning of the swing to come.

The first few inches of the backswing.

**ABOVE AND RIGHT:** Here the right leg is twisting and the foot rolling too much.

## IT'S A ONE-PIECE MOVEMENT

Hands and arms should begin to move away from the ball, and shoulders turn, as a single, integrated movement. If you allow the hands to take over right away, as feels natural, they will dominate all through, and ruin your swing.

Very soon, your hips begin to follow the turning movements of your shoulders. Continue your turn with the ultimate aim of presenting your back to your target; your hips won't turn as much, finishing at about 45 degrees.

Now I'm not suggesting that you equip yourself with a protractor and measure off 45 degrees. Things are actually simpler than that. This is because the turn is made around the axle that is your right leg. Though it isn't rigid, and remains flexed, as in your stance position, it must not move, or that sweet swing of yours will become a sway, and you may well find yourself hopelessly off balance.

If you maintain the position of your right leg, then that 45 degree angle of your hips follows automatically. They will simply not be able to move any further.

**ABOVE AND BELOW:** Stages of the backswing.

**ABOVE AND RIGHT:** A good leg position at the top of the backswing.

# WHAT HAPPENS TO THE WRISTS?

Your wrists have to flex at some point in your backswing. This can happen either naturally, or as a deliberate movement, in three different ways. They are:

(1) Flexing can be delayed until the end of the backswing, the last real movement in fact. There is one very clear advantage in this, in that the player is encouraged to make a full shoulder turn, and can keep that in mind as the main backswing thought. Only when the full shoulder turn has been made are the wrists allowed to break.

(2) This, somewhat confusingly, is the exact reverse of (1). The wrist-break is completed early, once the one-piece beginning of the backswing is accomplished.

This method, apparently, does nothing to help the golfer make the full shoulder turn, but it gets the wrist-break out of the way early, and is easier to perform at this point when the swing is still slow. If left to the last moment, the argument goes, the wrist-break can become involved in the transition from backswing to downswing.

(3) Flexing can be continuous and gradual, carried out right throughout the backswing. This is, perhaps, the most natural method, but it doesn't give the golfer any key swing thoughts to hang on to.

Early wrist break – sometimes called 'setting the angle early'.

Too much lift of the left heel.

This stance is better.

## THE FEET

Although you are very likely to have spikes in the soles of your shoes, you certainly shouldn't be rooted to the ground by them. The pull exerted by your backswing will cause both feet to roll naturally, and it's quite likely that the left side and heel of your left foot will leave the ground. This is fine, and helps to give freedom to the swing, but your heel shouldn't be allowed to leave the ground completely. If it does, then you are lifting away from the ball, and not swinging.

Your right foot will roll very much less, as a result of the transfer of weight from the inside to the outside of the foot.

Spiked shoes should not prevent your feet from rolling during the backswing.

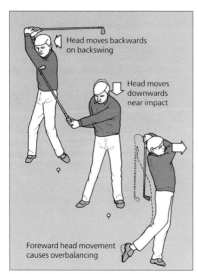

Keeping the head still during the swing is one of the novice's biggest problems. The above are the three most common head movement faults.

Labels in image: Head moves backwards on backswing; Head moves downwards near impact; Foreward head movement causes overbalancing

## THE HEAD

No golfer can execute a full swing without moving the head. Many golfers have *thought* that they could, and although it's impossible, it's certainly something to aim at.

Good players do move their heads, but it's a relatively small movement which takes place in two directions. Perhaps the head moves a couple of inches backwards, increasing by an inch or more by impact, and a couple of inches downwards by the time the club strikes the ball. Even so, teachers tell their pupils not to move their heads and may, for example, place a hand on the head to check the amount of movement.

In an ideal world, the head would remain completely steady, but in practical terms, the turning of the shoulders creates a pull on the neck which is transferred into a head movement. Perhaps a robot could do it, but the human frame just isn't flexible enough.

So we must learn to live with it.

To start with the obvious, golf becomes a much more difficult game if your head turns so much that you can't see the ball when you are at the top of your backswing. Demands on a golfer's hand and eye co-ordination are quite severe enough without adding any more.

If you find that this is happening, then you must shorten the length of your backswing. The point at which the pull on neck muscles becomes extreme depends entirely on the body doing the swinging. While some people have to stop short, others can swing back well beyond the horizontal without untoward problems.

One thing you can do is to turn your head a little to the right in your initial set-up. Jack Nicklaus, in fact, makes a very definite turn of his head to the right, just before swinging back. He's got that head turn out of the way before the stroke commences.

Please – don't be too dispirited about my comments regarding unavoidable head movement. A blind man can play very good golf, providing he begins with clubhead to ball. In the same way, our memories do enable us to find the ball, even with the eyes shut.

Indeed, there have been very great golfers who played with far too much head movement. It used to be said of the great Walter Hagen, for example, that he 'began with a sway and ended with a lunge'. Among modern champions, Curtis Strange is renowned for the amount of sway in his swing.

So far, we have been considering the effects of lateral head movement. But your head can move up and down, as well as from side to side. Your head shouldn't be lifted by your arms and shoulder movement. If it is, you're not *turning* at the top of your backswing, but simply *lifting* your arms up.

Lifting the arms.

The Nicklaus head position before swinging.

In fact, you're not getting a swing at all. It's wise to check on this, either in a mirror, or by asking an onlooker.

On the other hand, your head may move forward as you come into the ball, which probably means you are throwing your body at the ball rather than the clubhead. Most good players involuntarily lower their heads a little in the impact zone, and their heads also move backwards. If they didn't, the golfer would lose balance and fall over!

A full backswing.

Fred Couples at the 1989 Ryder Cup.

# SWING PLANES

Now we must visualize your swing plane. To do this, imagine a straight line, drawn from the base of your neck to the ball when you have taken up your stance. Alternatively, you could think of a large wheel in that same plane, with the base of your neck as the hub. The rim of that wheel would pass through the ball and extend to the same distance in the opposite direction.

As you stand to the ball, everything – clubhead, hands, arms, are inside the wheel. And should stay there, on backswing, downswing and through swing.

Let's look at some errors which send the swing outside that imaginary wheel, and see what results.

(1) At the very beginning of the take-away, the club can swing away from the body. Lee Trevino does this, as do many others. While there is little direct harm in this, it does add the complication of having to bring the club back on track.

(2) The arms may lift much later in the backswing, when the hands are at about shoulder level. In this case, the player is either not turning their shoulders properly, or simply doesn't have enough flexibility to swing properly.

However, the player has to get that clubhead well back, so the only thing to do is to *lift* it there.

It's just about impossible to recover from this position, and the clubhead is now outside your imaginary wheel. Admittedly, Miller Barber and James Bruen managed to avert disaster by looping the clubhead back inside the wheel, and did it very well, too, but for the average golfer it makes consistent play almost impossible.

If you don't loop back inside the wheel, what happens? Probably one of three things.

The ball may curve rapidly to the right, because you have cut across it from right to left, with the clubface more or less square-on to the ball.

On the other hand, the ball may go left, because while your swing path was satisfactory enough, you have hit it with the face more or less closed. In extreme cases, you can even endanger your left foot!

It could fly absolutely straight, in which case you have performed a bit of magic. You have cut across the ball from right to left, with your clubhead slightly closed. A classic case of two wrongs making a right. Even so, you'll lose distance, because the clubhead momentum isn't flowing straight down the target line.

All things considered, you'll agree that it must be simpler to deliver the clubhead to the ball along the right path; the deviations caused by the clubface not arriving square to the target line cause enough problems, anyway.

Arc of the clubhead during the swing.

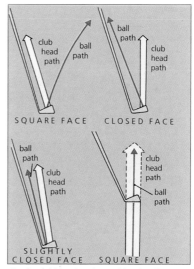

Results of clubhead moving outside swing plane.

This swing is too flat and is likely to create a pull or hook shot.

This swing is too upright and is likely to create the dreaded slice.

# FLAT AND UPRIGHT SWING PLANES

If people criticize your swing as being either "too upright" or 'too flat', you can probably ignore them. Ben Hogan and Jack Nicklaus would be in most people's list of the best six golfers ever, yet Hogan had a flat swing, and Nicklaus is upright. But both kept inside that imaginary wheel.

There are, however, extremes which must be avoided. If you're flat, don't let your plane get below shoulder level, and if upright, it's as well to avoid letting your backswing hit you on the head.

It seems to me that Nicklaus now swings on a considerably flatter plane than he used to – and will probably suffer less back trouble. On the other hand, Nicklaus's upright swing was hugely influential, simply because anything done by the world's best golfer is widely imitated. Consider the Vardon grip, in its day, or the sight of Bobby Jones playing his full shots with his feet close together.

It isn't wise, however, to imitate the great players too slavishly. While Vardon's grip was obviously impeccable,

**ABOVE LEFT AND RIGHT:** Average plane, different viewpoints.

Jones's stance would simply demand too much from the average golfer's balancing abilities. Similarly, the Hogan and Nicklaus swing planes, flat and upright respectively, are extremes, and unlikely to suit most golfers.

In 1990, Nick Faldo established himself, for a while anyway, as the world's greatest golfer. In spite of the fact that he stands well over average height, he is a man who can safely be imitated. His plane is not at either extreme, and he has probably given more thought to his swing than any other player.

At the beginning of his career, his swing was an aesthetic pleasure to observe – a loop at the top of a swing can give more impression of grace and rhythm than the more functional up-and-down movement. But Faldo wanted to build himself the mechanical perfection he felt would withstand the enormous pressure of contending over the last few holes of a major tournament. You could say that he thought his 'Mark One' swing was good enough to win tournaments, but not the ones which guarantee a kind of immortality.

The rest is history.

# AT THE TOP

Let's assume that you have started back correctly, that you have remained in the correct plane, and that you have completed your swing away from the ball. Let's stop you there, for a moment, and examine the features which should be present once you have got the clubhead into, what the pro's call, 'the slot', and you are about to swing down to the ball.

(1) If your grip is a good one, the face of your club should be parallel to the target line – not open or closed to it.

(2) Your shoulders should be turned as much as your own flexibility allows. Some can't quite achieve a complete right-angle, others manage a little more. Failing to complete that shoulder turn is one of golf's most common faults, partly because many golfers are too hand-conscious. They get the club up there on high all right, but only by pushing upwards with the hands and lifting their arms in order to do so.

(3) The fullness of your swing determines where your toe points. Perhaps the ideal is 'at the ground', which happens when the length of your backswing positions the shaft

In the slot.

Checking angle of shaft and clubhead position.

Checking wrist-break.

Good position at the top.

A good shoulder turn.

Again, a good shoulder turn.

parallel to the ground. As I say, this is ideal, but many players have played golf superbly with a much shorter swing: remember Doug Sanders, who, they used to quip, 'could swing in a phone box'?

Many others travel on past the horizontal. This is perfectly acceptable, and perhaps even beneficial, because the player then has more time and space to develop clubhead speed in a relatively leisurely way.

But extra length can be achieved, even with a swing fault. Players can allow the clubhead to drop when they have reached the effective end of the backswing, probably in an attempt to achieve the maximum distance from the ball. Dropping the clubhead in this way, however, achieves nothing, and provides less control over the club.

(4) Hand position. It's possible to make a full shoulder turn, but still end up with the hands only a little above shoulder height at the end of the backswing. This isn't a disaster, but it does result in a shorter swing arc. If you become conscious of stretching away from the ball, then this certainly involves the arms, giving width to the swing, and placing the hands naturally well above shoulder height. Remember, though, this must be as the result of a swing, and not a lift.

ABOVE LEFT AND RIGHT: Has the clubhead been allowed to drop?

Low hands.

High hands.

Back to something like the address position before the hands come in.

Body returns to address position before hands and arms.

# BACK TO THE BALL

The first few inches of the backswing are the most vital moments of a golf swing, but even when this and all the rest of the backswing are performed to perfection, disaster can still follow. Your backswing only sets you up with the best chance of carrying out the downswing successfully.

So let's start with some 'don'ts'.

(1) As we've seen, some golfers are much too 'hand-conscious'. For them, it's quite natural to throw the hands at the ball as the main movement of the downswing. This may be effective in a game such as table tennis, where there's relatively little body movement in making a shot, but it doesn't work for golf.

(2) The shoulders contain some of the most powerful muscles in the body, so it seems natural, to some people, to try to make the most of them. They do this by heaving their shoulders at the ball, in an attempt to gain clubhead speed, but succeed only in getting themselves out of plane. The usual result is a clubhead path across the target line, producing a slice or a pull hook.

(3) Swinging back at the ball with the feeling that it's your arms which really count is a lesser disaster than the two previous faults. You might even manage to play passable golf with this swing, while letting the lower body take care of itself. But you won't play *good* golf.

The downswing must be led by the lower body – hips, legs, and let's not forget the feet. Golfers tend to hold key thoughts about how to initiate the journey back to the ball, some, for example, 'kicking off' with the right foot. Others think of turning the hips back towards the ball, and a few concentrate on beginning to straighten the left leg. That's all very well, but such a thought must not be taken in isolation. Feet, legs and hips make another of those one-piece movements, working rhythmically and in unison.

These parts of the anatomy should have returned to something like their position at the address, even before the hands and arms come into play at all, and during the time it takes the shoulders to make about half a turn.

This lower-body movement is common to all good players. You'll never see a competent golfer with a poor leg action, or an incompetent player with a good one. The poor player is far too preoccupied with thoughts about their hands, or about heaving with their shoulders: the legs are ignored and a very badly balanced and ineffective swing is the result. So, I repeat, the lower body must lead the downswing, and is the basis of a golf swing.

Meanwhile, what *has* happened to the hands and arms?

They should have remained passive, but that lower-body

**TOP LEFT AND RIGHT AND ABOVE:** Good and relaxed leg action, different viewpoints.

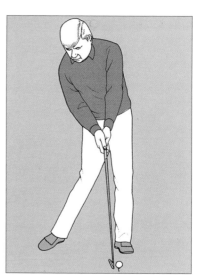

Clubhead and hands at impact, increasing the loft of an iron with the ball forward in the stance.

**TOP AND ABOVE:** Virtually all hands and arms from now on.

movement back to the ball does have an effect, namely to pull the arms down to approximately hip level. By themselves, the arms do nothing at all.

But their moment is coming! The rest of the down and through swing is virtually all hands and arms, and they provide by far the greatest part of clubhead speed.

Even at this late point in the swing, even when everything has gone very well indeed, your action can still go fatally wrong. And the crucial point is the position of the left wrist at impact.

So many poor players produce a flicking movement in that final moment. When they meet the ball, the left wrist is already flexed, forcing the palm of the hand to face the floor.

The left wrist should remain firm, with the back of the hand facing the target, and the palm facing to the rear, just as it does in the address position. Let's think of what happens if it does flex in the impact area of your swing.

You can try it out for yourself in slow motion. Two things are immediately apparent.

If you are using an iron, the blade will rapidly increase in loft, and just as certainly, it will become more open. All golfers who allow the wrists to flex too early are habitual slicers – unless they grip the club in an extremely shut position – and, usually, they will hit the ball very high, because they have turned the loft of a 5-iron into, say, a 7-iron.

From time to time, such golfers will play quite good golf, and on a good day, their timing of the wrist-break will be fairly consistent. But the slice and loss of distance will surely still be there. 'All right,' you may say, 'that can be compensated by using straight-faced irons, more so than should be needed for a shot of that length. So it doesn't matter in the least.'

Quite so. But you won't be in the least pleased about your loss of distance with driver and fairway woods.

Far more important, how can you hope to meet the ball with the same amount of wrist break each time? No. That firm left wrist is the recipe for consistency. Let the lesson be – the left wrist must still be in the address position at impact.

The left wrist flexed too early.

This is how it should be. Left arms and club still in a straight line.

An elevated tee.

**TOP AND ABOVE:** Shoulders move through about 90 degrees.

A poor turn.

Heaving with the shoulders.

## THE SHOULDERS

There is nothing at all complicated about the correct movement of the shoulders. They turn from a position parallel with the target line at address, through 90 degrees, or more, at the top of the backswing, and back to the address position at impact.

This is easier said than done. In the heat of competition, you'll often hear a pro bemoan 'I didn't make a good turn', meaning that he didn't complete a full shoulder turn so that he got his back to the target. This will almost certainly have meant that his shoulders were open when he got back to the ball. Instead they should have been, once more, parallel to the target line.

The poor golfer's problems, however, are far worse. The shoulders, too, make that incomplete turn, and almost every time, the power is seen as coming from the upper body. They lash too early with their hands, heave with their shoulders, and find themselves far too open at the moment of impact. The swing path is disastrously across the ball, right to left, and the result is a slice, often quite severe, if the clubface is square or open at impact, and a fairly sharp left pull if it is closed.

# SOURCES OF CLUBHEAD SPEED

I suggest that, at this point, you dissect your swing, bit by bit, with all the movements carried out correctly. Try the lower body – feet, legs, hips – first. There doesn't seem to be much speed from that area, does there?

Now the shoulders and back. A little more? But not much. So far, you have seen all those powerful thigh, back and shoulder muscles provide very little in the way of clubhead speed, though, admittedly, they do help. In the main, as I have already stressed, they provide the mechanical basis so that the hands and arms can lash the clubhead through the target line. They are vital in moving heavy weights – but a golf club isn't exactly heavy.

Primarily, to hit a long ball, what is needed is the ability to accelerate a light weight – a golf clubhead and shaft. And that's done by a combination of hand and arm speed.

**CLOCKWISE:** Complete swing sequence.

# TEE SHOTS

For most club golfers, the aim is to hit the ball as far as possible. There are few who don't boast, on return to the clubhouse, that 'I reached the 320-yard 14th off the tee today!' Or 'Dammit, if I didn't put my tee shot into that stream across the 12th. Must be all of 300 yards!'

Yet there is little doubt that Greg Norman let in Mark Calcavecchia to win the 1989 British Open at Royal Troon simply by driving the ball too far.

You have to decide if these bunkers are in range.

Could you drive straight between the avenue of trees in the distance? Better to play short of them with an iron.

There is very little room for error on this tee. An accurate drive is needed between the trees, which are waiting for those wayward shots.

On the last hole of the four-hole play-off, Norman unleashed one of his thunderboits and reached a bunker that everyone had found to be out of range all week. With that shot went the Championship, yet Greg had been warned that he might reach it if the adrenalin was in full flow. It was Jack Nicklaus who had said so, and he was proved right. If Norman had played a 3-wood he might well have become Champion for the second time.

So, unless your priority is telling a good tale in the clubhouse, rather than arriving there with a good score under your belt, the purpose of the tee shot is not to hit far enough to reach a bunker or a water hazard.

'But,' you could argue 'there aren't many lay-up tee shots on an average golf course.' That's true. Apart from sand, such hazards as water, belts of rough, or the occasional quarry, are much more likely to be intended to threaten a second shot. Only the exceptionally long drivers are menaced by them.

So we all want to hit the tee shot as far as we can, but that distance can still be a disadvantage, and I don't mean just because we might reach trouble.

Before playing your tee shot, you should always think first about where the green is. Then go further. Can you see the day's flag position? If you know the course well, where do you want to hit and stop on the green? Perhaps to give yourself an uphill putt?

**ABOVE AND RIGHT:** If your tee shot reaches here, you'll have to take a penalty drop.

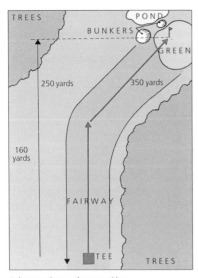

A short tee shot to a better position.

From the right of this fairway you wouldn't have to try to draw your second shot around the trees.

When you've analyzed these matters, it will become obvious that the shot to the green (or the second shot on a par 5) isn't always best played from the centre of the fairway, however long your tee shot. If, for example, the green slopes only a little from right to left, you'll have a far better chance of stopping your ball predictably if you are coming in from the left, because of the increased bite you'll get when pitching into an upslope, however slight.

On the other hand, if the flag is set on the extreme left of the green, you may need to change your thinking. Coming in from the left will give you no room to work in, and from this angle, you'll have to pitch short, possibly catch up in some rough. In that case, your ball will not behave quite as predictably as if you can land directly on the green. So, you'll decide to discount the downslope (there will be plenty of green to play with when the flag is on the left), and play your tee shot down the right of the fairway.

If you are on the left of this fairway, you have to play for the flag over water.

The main problem here is out of bounds along the left.

You wouldn't want to play to this flag from well left.

But you haven't finished thinking yet. Next, you will need to consider the immediate surrounds of the green. Are there any bunkers, or other hazards? Almost certainly there are. And remember, such threats to your score aren't just sand and water. You'll obviously be looking out for potentially hazardous trees and bushes, but also note whether the ground falls away sharply, either to left or right of the green. If it does, then a chip or short pitch will be much less likely to finish close to the hole. Generally speaking, it is sensible to come in from the side which presents fewest problems between you and the flag.

Only after you have analyzed these, and any other, problems should you consider playing your tee shot. A 160-yard tee shot down the right, for example, could leave you with a better line in to the flag than a 250-yard drive along the left.

Remember the golden rule: A good drive sets you up to play the rest of the hole. Viewed in isolation, it's worth very little, apart from the exhilaration that comes with hitting long and high.

## PROBLEMS FROM THE TEE

So far we have looked at problems, in the area of the green, which need to be considered before a tee shot is played. However, many golfers don't get that far in their thinking, being far more concerned with immediate problems – those directly facing the tee shot.

LEFT: Keep your eye on the ball when there's water in front of the tee.

With the sea to the left, and gorse on the right,
you've got to aim accurately.

With dangers like this on either side you must
hit the fairway with your tee shot. It will cost you
dearly if you don't.

Arnold Palmer watches Christy O'Connor drive off.

The one which most concerns every golfer, at any level, is the presence of trouble either side of the fairway. Let's imagine that we are playing a hole with water on the left, and out of bounds' on the right. Just to make things more interesting, let's also suppose that the fairway is humpbacked, like the 10th on the Open Championship course at Turnberry. In fact, let's imagine that a drive which is only a fraction off dead center will run you towards trouble, particularly when the ground is hard, whether you err from left to right.

Doesn't worry you in the least? Driving well today? Fine. By all means, blaze away. But if doubts do creep in, don't let them cramp your swing. Remember that the backswing must always be completed. You'll find that the ball tends to go straighter when you swing full out: don't be tempted to hold something in reserve in the vain hope of gaining greater control. That *never* works.

Let's now be a little more realistic, even if slightly more pessimistic. Let's say you haven't been driving badly, but aren't completely confident of getting a really straight one away.

Immediately, you should be thinking in terms of leaving the driver in the bag – which doesn't mean automatically reaching for the 3-wood. Many club golfers never even

Checking alignment to aim away from out of bounds along the right.

Hitting left.

consider hitting an iron to the fairway, but the pros think very differently.

What will the safe shot be on our imaginary terror hole? Basically, the only way to hold this fairway is to hit one of the upslopes with either a slight fade or draw. You should be thinking 5-iron, denying yourself the pleasure this time of the long, straight drive, realizing that it is all too likely to cost you strokes.

Let's now cut our tee shot problems by 50%, removing our imaginary 'out of bounds' area on the right, but retaining the water on the left. When your confidence is peaking, you can probably ignore it. When it isn't, take up your stance on the left of the teeing area, and play away from the trouble. By doing this you've given yourself a 45-degree margin of error, and even quite a sizeable hook probably won't find the water. Teeing up on the left in this way makes the big difference, and gives you a much better chance of avoiding trouble than simply aiming down the right of the fairway.

**TOP, CENTER AND ABOVE:** If you're confident enough that you can draw the ball, you can aim at the out of bounds and watch your ball drift back again.

**ABOVE:** You have to aim right of center to cope with this sloping fairway when the ground is hard.

# DRIVING TO A DOGLEG

When playing a dogleg par 4, you'll often have the option of carrying the angle. You need to consider what length of carry is required, and how severely you'll be punished if you fail. Success, however, will often mean a relatively short pitch to the green and a birdie opportunity. For long hitters, the reward for carrying a dogleg is a chance of reaching the green in one.

If you decide that you can't make the carry, or that the risks are too great, then you should be thinking of the right placement for your tee shot. The degree of accuracy required rules out the driver, and indeed it's often all too possible to run out of fairway and finish in the rough.

As before, consider greenside problems and flat position, and set yourself up to reach the best second shot you can.

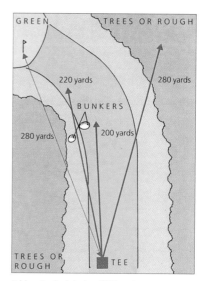

Driving at a short dogleg of 350 yards.

# THE BEST SHAPE OF SHOT

Most professionals aim to drive with fade or draw, calculating that one consistent pattern gives them more fairway to work with. The fader, for example, can aim a little into the rough on the left. Always providing the fade 'takes', they then have a large margin for error before running into trouble on their right, when the fade becomes an outright slice.

The fade has one great advantage for players ranging from the great to the merely competent. Fade spin is greater than draw spin, and increases the chances of holding the fairway. Even quite ordinary players don't seem to have days which are quite as bad as those who draw the ball. Many pro's who prefer consistency to absolute length quite deliberately settle on this type of shot: Jack Nicklaus, Nick Faldo and Ben Hogan (who wasn't a great player until he defeated his hook) are among the champions who favor this method.

However, there does seem to be a tendency, these days, for professionals to favor the draw. Extra length is a formidable advantage for consistent players. The very long driver can find themselves playing mid-irons into par 5's and, in still air, even quite long par 4's can be covered with a drive and a pitch. Your big driver is obviously far more likely to place those kinds of shot close to the flag than the golfer who is hitting woods or long irons from much greater distances.

This was the approach of the young Jack Nicklaus. Jack, himself, wrote that his method was to power it away with his seige-gun driving and then 'slop it on the green'.

Many of today's players would approve, although they wouldn't necessarily use the word 'slop'. They know perfectly

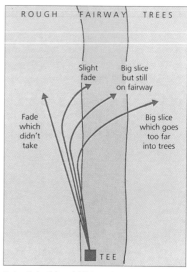

Fade, aiming left and drifting right.

The 'rough' comes in all different forms and this is one of the worst. The clubhead gets entangled with the grass and weeds on both the takeaway and again at the moment of impact.

well that the long tee shot is far more likely to finish off the fairway, but today's improved equipment combines with fast hand action to hold the green from poor lies in the rough.

For club players, the draw shape is likely to lead to problems. When you're not quite on top form, that little tail away to the left when the ball is well on its way stops behaving itself, and every tee shot becomes a quick hook. Extra distance is replaced by acute embarrassment.

Neither is the average club player very effective from the rough. Playing far less often than the pro, they haven't acquired anything like the wrist strength (I recall Peter Alliss telling me how much smaller his wrists became when he gave up tournament golf), and cannot get the clubhead through the rough and also retain control.

Overall, I must still come down on the side of the fade, but it is worth emphasizing that a fade isn't a slice. The slice immediately starts going right, and continues in a parabola. The fade spends most of its time straight, and only moves left to right late in flight.

# DRIVING IN WIND

### TAIL WINDS

Let's assume you want maximum distance. Hitting the ball
low will do little actual harm, but your ball will be flying
below the full strength of the wind, and will not get maximum
benefit from it. You therefore need to get the ball up into the
air, and let the wind work on it. If you naturally hit a high ball,
then all well and good. If not, you might start thinking in
terms of the greater loft of a fairway wood.

### HEADWINDS

Driving into the wind is a far more difficult proposition. The
first thing to do is to avoid fighting it. It is very tempting to
think that the wind is going to take 80 yards off your drive so
that you must hit it harder, but that approach is fraught with
danger.

For a start, this will destroy your rhythm, just at the time
when the wind has already adversely affected your balance.

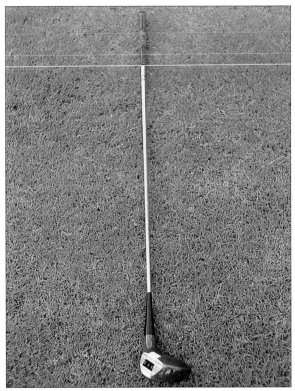

A persimmon head driver.

Ball on a high tee.

And also forward in the stance.

Even if you do bring it off, you'll still achieve precisely nothing.

That drive which would have travelled a delightful distance in still air will have been very well struck with high swing speed and will therefore have more backspin, as does any well-struck shot. Consequently, a harder drive won't give you increased distance, but greater backspin, causing your ball to soar upwards into the wind. Certainly, it will have travelled a great distance when it eventually comes back to earth, but most of that additional length will be up and down, rather than forward.

Obviously, the ball has to be kept low. There are several ways of doing this, including the one used by Seve Ballesteros and other tournament pro's.

In this method, the ball is teed up higher than usual, accepting the risk of getting under the ball, causing it to fly directly upwards off the top of the clubface. The ball is also placed a little further forward in the stance than is the norm. The aim is then to make contact on the upswing, the idea being to hit up at the ball, thereby reducing backspin and thus preventing the ball flying upwards as far as it might have done if it had been teed at normal height.

A low tee and the ball back in the stance.

Normal height of tee and ball position.

Another approach is quite the reverse. The ball is moved back a couple of inches in the stance and a low tee is used. The club is gripped a little lower, by a couple of inches, and the idea is to hold a mental image of the hands well ahead of the clubhead, which is pulled through the ball. If you try this, don't hit full out, and keep the wrists relatively inactive. Aim for a precise stroke, rather than a hard one.

### SIDE WINDS

Again, there are two very different ways of approaching this problem. One is to play your normal shot, but allow for the effect of the wind. Then simply allow 10, 20 or even 50 yards of drift, according to wind speed. Also remember that a side wind reduces your distance, although the major effect is on your direction.

This is the easiest way to counter a side wind, but players with the skill to shape their shots either way can handle the problem differently. In a left-to-right wind, play a draw and, when the wind is coming into your body, play a fade. Shape of shot and wind effects then cancel each other out. The professionals call it 'holding the ball into the wind'.

A poor tee shot can land you in all sorts of trouble.

## HITTING IRONS TO THE FAIRWAY

One of the biggest thrills in golf is hitting the ball a very long way. But an even bigger one is a good score. And that means thinking as well as hitting.

When playing a tight course many professionals make little use of the driver, often only using it when they really do need the distance, say, on the par 5's and long par 4's. Otherwise their thinking is that it's much better to play the next shot from the fairway than from the trees, or after taking a penalty drop from the water.

Here's where the 1-iron comes into play. It's a difficult club, except in skilled hands, however, and many club golfers don't feel confident until they have something with the loft of a 4- or 5-iron in their hands. If that's your feeling, then use a more lofted iron. After all, the idea is to play a safe shot to the fairway, so there's no sense in taking a longer iron – you might even be more effective with your normal driver.

I know – you lose the pleasure of a long drive, but there's a different sort of enjoyment in placing your tee shot precisely, and knowing that you've used brain instead of brawn.

Irons also come into play when you're not sure whether you might reach trouble – sand, water, rough – with your driver. If you know you can't carry a hazard but fear you might reach it, then the obvious decision is to play short.

**ABOVE LEFT AND RIGHT:** Taking an iron from the tee.

Why not lay up short of the water, rather than risk a difficult carry?

## FAIRWAY WOODS FROM THE TEE

If you have a favorite 3- or 4-wood, one with which you are confident you can play safe, you could often use it as an alternative to an iron from the tee. Indeed, as there is little loss of distance involved, a wood with some loft might lower your score, if played throughout your round.

During the 1990 British Open at St Andrews, Nick Faldo often chose a 2-wood, and such past champions as Peter Thomson and Bobby Locke often didn't even carry a driver, in the interests of keeping on the fairway.

## HOW TO DRAW AND FADE

In this section, I'm going to assume that the basic shape of your shot is straight. If you are, for example, an habitual slicer, don't think that you can cure your fault by tacking this

The Trevino set-up.

An open clubface at address is likely to produce a slice instead of a fade.

A slightly closed clubface will probably cause the hook as opposed to the intended draw.

or that draw technique on to a fundamentally poor grip, swing plane or stance.

The general technique of Lee Trevino points some lessons. He has won six majors – US Open and British Open twice each, and a couple of PGA Championships, as well as a whole host of other tournaments. Now entering his fifties he still remains a major force and number one on the Seniors Tour.

The young Trevino hooked the ball, but having watched Ben Hogan, another natural hooker, decided that the fade was the pattern of shot for him. One of Hogan's basic recipes was to move his left hand slightly counter-clockwise, Trevino however, didn't wish to change his grip, which features the so-called 'strong' left-hand grip, with perhaps three knuckles showing. Although his right-hand grip is more conventional, with the 'V' pointing towards his right shoulder, it is still much stronger than used by most pro's today. This means that, at the top of his swing, his clubface is very shut – at right angles to the target – rather than parallel with it. For most of us, if the swing were normal, this ought to produce a pull or hook, or both together!

To fade the ball, Trevino does various things. In the first place, he stands at an angle of about 45 degrees open to his target line. If you saw a player with this kind of stance on your

**TOP LEFT AND RIGHT, AND ABOVE:** Open, square and closed with an iron.

club's practice ground, you'd dismiss them as hopeless.

He also stands with his ball, apparently, too far forward – just about opposite his left toe. These two positions would guarantee a slice for most of us, but Trevino's shut clubface makes all the difference.

Now we come to the swing back to the ball. Trevino leads strongly with his legs, slides his hips along the target line, and keeps his hands dead. His attack on the ball is almost entirely a pull, coming from the left side of his body, and continuing after impact. The result is a swing across the ball and a clubface which is still square on: only if he wants to draw the ball does Trevino let his hands into the action, closing the face a little at impact.

There could be hints here for the club golfer, but the total method would surely be disastrous. It only works for Lee Trevino because other movements in his swing are so extreme that they make it relatively easy for him to detect which part of his swing mechanism has gone wrong.

By comparison, the Jack Nicklaus system for fading and drawing the ball is simplicity itself. He goes for complete orthodoxy, hitting a straight shot and making just one adjustment. He sets his club in his grip so that the blade is slightly open for the fade or closed for the draw – and, obviously enough, he also adjusts his aim to allow for drift.

To the Nicklaus method for the fade we can add other touches:

(1) Like Trevino, set your ball further forward in your stance.
(2) Again, like Trevino, open your stance.
(3) Weaken your left-hand grip, but be wary of the fact that changing your grip can feel uncomfortable. Nicklaus maintains the same grip, adjusting only the club.
(4) Keep the hands quiet, using a pulling movement through the ball.

To obtain draw, simply do the reverse, although there is perhaps one exception. Closing the stance isn't advisable for most people, probably giving the feeling that your left side is in the way and inhibiting the full swing.

## USES OF DRAW AND FADE FROM THE TEE

(1) If a fairway slopes strongly, especially if that slope is towards a hazard, a shot drifting in the opposite direction should help you hold the fairway, even when the ground is hard.
(2) The shape of a hole usually means that a shot of the same shape is very useful. Let's consider a par 4, swinging gently from right to left, but not a sharply angled dogleg. A straight tee shot will do well enough, but a draw will follow the fairway

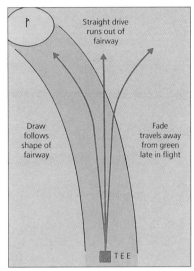

Following the shape of a fairway.

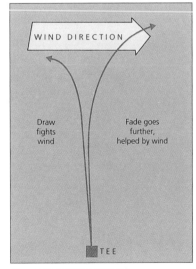

Draw and fade in left to right wind.

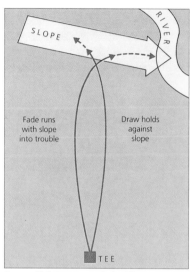

Draw and fade from tee to a sloping fairway.

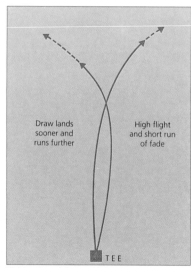

Flight and run of draw and fade.

curve, in effect, giving a longer drive. A fade, in these circumstances, will end by almost travelling away from the green, leading to a longer second shot.

(3) You can also use the wind for greater length. If, for example, you are driving with the wind blowing on your back (left to right), a fade will be helped along, while a draw would be fighting the wind. However, this only applies in light to medium winds: trying to make use of a gale in this way is far too risky.

It is just as likely that your ball will be swept away, so it is better to use draw or fade to combat a strong wind, obtaining a more controlled tee shot.

(4) The fade gives a relatively high tee shot, the draw a lower one. The fade stops relatively quickly on landing, the draw lands more quickly and is likely to run. You can therefore use the draw for maximum length when the ground is firm or hard, and the fade to a soft fairway. In the second case, there would be little run, and a fade carries further through the air.

## PRACTICING YOUR DRIVING

I always think that the term 'driving range' is dangerous. It encourages golfers to take out a bucket of balls and hit them away, flat out. The phrase 'practice range' is preferable, implying that you can use all the clubs in the bag, and not just the driver.

Hitting at maximum power all the time can lead you off course, especially if you don't do that when you are out on the course. It can also destroy your rhythm.

So let's start with a general 'don't'. Don't stand there on a driving range or practice ground and simply hit out. Professionals always try to keep something in reserve, because precision and rhythm are far more important than the chance to occasionally hit an exceptionally long ball.

Here's what you should do:
■ *Avoid hitting at maximum power.*

Always try to keep balanced and rhythmic, and limit yourself to what feels like about 80% effort.
■ *Always select a target to aim at.*

Don't merely try out your full swing. Your tee shot will always be aimed at a small area of fairway, so reflect this in your practice.
■ *Vary the shape of your shot.*

Left-to-right, right-to-left, high and low. You won't, for example, be able to play a left-to-righter in the real life of the golf course by magic. You have to learn how to do these things in practice.
■ *Learn the distance you hit the ball.*

Ignore short mis-hits and long balls alike. The good

The player will want to avoid bunkers, the humpy ground right and left and also be along the left side of the fairway for the best line to the flag.

Don't just use the driver from the tee.

average is what you should have in mind. Your driving is good when that length is consistent, so that there is only about 20 yards between your longest and shortest balls.

■ *Don't practice only driving, just before a serious round.*

This is when you should be concentrating on warming up, and on touch and rhythm. Just hitting with the driver alone won't help your game.

■ *Only practice with driver alone when that club is giving you trouble.*

Most practice sessions are more valuable using all, or most, of the clubs in your bag. If it *is* to be the driver, don't practice too long. The energy you exert can rapidly tire you. At least pause for rest and thought between shots, and always think about what you are aiming to achieve with each one. Swishing ball after ball away without pause may be good exercise, but it isn't golf.

But perhaps there is one exception. Jimmy Demaraet once watched Ben Hogan playing a very, very long session of 3-woods. To Demaraet they all seemed to be excellent shots, so he approached Hogan and asked Hogan what he was seeking to achieve. Said Hogan:

'I'm trying to see how I play the club when I'm tired.'

# EQUIPMENT

I n theory, any club can be used for a tee shot and in practice, nearly all of them are used from time to time. Only the putter can be said to be a total exception, even though you are allowed to use one.

In this book, however, I will deal only with some thoughts on choosing a driver. The other clubs are referred to elsewhere in *The Golf Instructor*.

## CHOOSING A DRIVER

Let there be no mistake about it. The driver is one of the most vital clubs to get right. Forget that tired old saying, 'You drive for show and putt for dough.' I know that there's a valid point being made. A 300 yard drive down the middle soon becomes unimportant if followed by a volley of poor shots and a three putt.

I say forget the phrase because a good tee shot enables you to play the rest of the hole. The brilliance of your putting will be worthless if you've previously hit three driver shots in a row out of bounds.

There are various tales of star golfers who have stayed faithful to the same driver for many years, perhaps even their whole career. Sam Snead is one example.

Immediately he appeared on the US Tour, he was successful and quickly recognized as a potentially great player, perhaps one already. But Sam knew he was likely to snap hooks his drives from time to time. Wild tee shots mean that a professional can't compete, except on good days. He wants to be sure that he can hit most of the fairways and that a really wild teeshot is going to be a rare occurrence, even when playing well below form.

Sam quickly found the answer when given quite a heavy club by Henry Picard. The extra weight, Sam thinks, helped him control his swing. He played with it for year upon year. It

Choosing the right equipment is as important as choosing the right line off the tee.

Drivers come in different sizes and weights. Furthermore the heads can
be made from metal, laminated maple or persimmon. But the important
thing, when buying one, is to make sure you feel comfortable with it.

was repaired again and again. Eventually, it was very likely a
substantially different club to swing than it had been
originally. But to Snead it was the same club. It gave him
confidence.

That's what you want most of all in a driver. There's no
easy way to find either the right club or confidence but, once
you have it, be like Snead and, even if you don't always use
the club, keep it by you.

A variety of factors will make up your ideal driver. As for
Sam Snead, weight is as important as anything. For every
golfer there is an ideal. No one can quite predict what it will
be. Thinking of length alone, this is the balance between
weight and clubhead speed. A heavier club swung at the same
speed as a lighter one will hit the ball further. The lighter club
will propel the ball further, however, if that lighter weight
means you can accelerate the clubhead at higher velocity.

Accuracy with the club is an entirely different matter.
Snead found that a heavier club helped him control his swing.
Others, however, using a heavy club might become wild off
the tee in their endeavors to accelerate a weight that is too
much for them.

The answer, of course, is that experimenting is
necessary. Try out used clubs, borrow others. Perhaps your
club professional will even tape new ones to avoid their being
marked. If you've the money, you can buy new ones from time

to time and part exchange them if they prove not to fit your swing.

As regards accuracy, the loft of the clubface is very important. A driver with an 8 degree loft will enable most players to get a longer tee shot than with a 12 degree loft. But the straighter-faced club is far less forgiving to a less than perfect strike. Most will find the 12 degree loft gives a more consistent result.

Length, but not accuracy and consistency, can also come, at least in part, from the materials used in the construction of the club.

Let's take the head first. Not so many years ago, there wasn't much choice. It was either solid persimmon or laminated wood. Many would say that in practice there wasn't much difference. Persimmon gave more delight to the eye but was more likely to crack than a laminated head. Greater or lesser distance was probably more a matter of the golfer's feelings about the club than any actual mechanical difference. Anyway, it was an insert that was brought into contact with the ball, not wood at all.

This brings us to the secret of the widespread acceptance of metal drivers. Do they cause the ball to leave the clubface with greater velocity? Many have found this to be

Plenty of room on the right, but watch the out of bounds on the left.

A light-weight steel shafted wood. The red laminated insert is there to assist in lining up the clubhead with the ball at address.

the case. If all other factors are equal, why should this be so? The answer has to be the harder material used.

Shafts are even more important. As regards length, the lightness of the shaft governs the weight that can be put into the head. The ideal is impossible – a shaft that weighs nothing at all. However, much work has gone into developing lighter shafts that still retain strength, but without increasing any tendency for them to twist while retaining desirable flex characteristics.

The first developments, after the triumph of the steel shaft over hickory, was in lighter weight steels, and since then all manner of materials have been used as a substitute for steel. Glass fiber, aluminum, titanium, carbon fiber and boron are a few examples.

How do average golfers decide? The answer is that they surely can't, but should seek professional advice and sound information. Discuss the matter with your club professional, who can analyze your swing and estimate, primarily, what weights and flex characteristics will suit you best. The old rule of thumb was that the stiff shaft ought to suit hard hitters while gentle swingers benefited from more flexible shafts. Hard hitters couldn't use flexible shafts because these flexed too much when swung fast. Gentle swingers felt they had a rigid pole in their hands when using a stiff shaft and lost the benefit of a 'kick' from a more flexible shaft. But there is more to it than that.

Where the club flexes is also important and has a strong influence on distance, accuracy and ball trajectory. The experienced eye of the club professional comes into play. They also have equipment which could help.

Even so, I feel it isn't an exact science and the golfer isn't a machine. In the end, it's not only the characteristics of the club but also how consistently the golfer reproduces his or her basic swing characteristics.

Provided the golf bag does its job it doesn't need to be as exotic as this one. However, if you can lay your hands on the clubs in this bag don't ever sell them, they're collectors' items.

# CARE OF YOUR DRIVER AND WOODS

If your 'woods' are made of metal, the heads need virtually no attention. I could go further and say that their performance won't be affected in any measurable degree however scratched and nicked they become. But you do need to give the faces of these clubs a few seconds' attention, to clean out the mud and crushed grass forced into the grooves. They help put backspin on the ball, which helps with control. If you obtained no backspin at all, actually an impossibility because of the loft on all clubs, the ball would dip rather than climb.

Sometimes a casual wipe-over will be sufficient, but crushed grass can be surprisingly tenacious. If this proves to be so, any brush with stiff bristles will accomplish the task.

A normal nail brush can be used for cleaning out the grooves on your clubs. Avoid using scourers, they could damage the club face.

A fine example of a golfer looking after his clubs and keeping them in good condition.

Again, a soft nail brush can be used for cleaning the grip on your club. However, scouring won't do any harm this time; in fact it will probably improve your hold on the grip.

A full-cord grip. The pattern is not there for decoration only, it is there to help you with the correct alignment of the clubhead at address.

An example of a wooden-headed club with a brass sole insert. Few of these clubs are used these days.

Take the head covers off to allow the clubs to dry naturally.

Woods that are actually made of wood can be cleaned in precisely the same way but the scratches and nicks are highly significant. They allow wet and damp to get through to the wood beneath the impermeable finish.

There are other areas to look out for on a wooden clubhead. The constant impact with ball and turf causes the finish to eventually crack around the face insert and the sole plate.

After playing in wet weather you should always allow the clubs to dry out naturally. Never leave head covers on. (These will often be wet as well, which means they make your clubheads wetter as well as preventing the air getting to them.) Of course the drying process will be speeded if you take the trouble to use a dry cloth on your heads.

However, these precautions don't solve the problem of damp getting into the clubs in the first place. There is only one solution. Examine them carefully from time to time and, when you notice any deterioration, have them re-finished in your professional's shop.

Modern shafts need no attention, though you may like to maintain their appearance, cosmetically speaking, by wiping them over with a damp cloth.

Grip condition is vital and I'm amazed how little attention the majority of golfers pay to them. In my opinion

The popular persimmon-headed driver, used by the majority of golfers.

The increasingly popular carbon fiber headed driver, which many of the top class players use these days.

. . . but, don't pick the carbon fiber driver just because your favorite golfer uses one. You must always choose one that you feel happy with.

The value of head covers were appreciated in the early days of golf as this cover shows. Its design was basic but its purpose was the same as the cover of today.

most modern golf grips are contemptible. I suspect they are designed to wear out as quickly as possible. You should, alas, be prepared to have them replaced by your professional every six months. This is because they quickly lose their essential 'tackiness', which helps you hold on to the club securely, and soon become smooth.

There is something you can do to restore the tacky feel. Your hands are always greasy and sometimes sweaty and dirty as well. An invisible deposit forms on the grip. Remove it by scrubbing with a brush, some detergent and soap. Rinse very thoroughly or else you will be worse off than when you began the operation. Soap and detergent are slippery substances.

As the grips deteriorate, this simple treatment becomes less effective. I'm afraid, for the clubs used the most frequently, it will last only one round of golf.

The days before the mass production market; a pair of craftsman made woods.

The persimmon head can be found on most woods these days but this one, with the boron shaft, is gradually making its presence felt

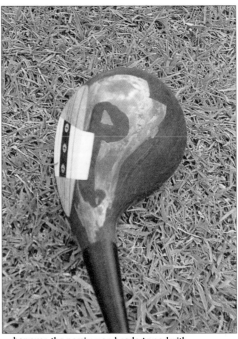

... however, the persimmon-headed wood with steel shaft remains the most popular wood amongst club golfers.

Another modern-day innovation is the ceramic headed 'wood'. Those shown here have the boron shafts.

Golf clubs don't have to be this expensive, but if you want the latest in golfing technology then you have to pay for it.

Choosing woods can be a hazardous task as this
vast selection in the pro's shop shows.

Despite the vast choice available, many
players still trust the laminated maple wood.

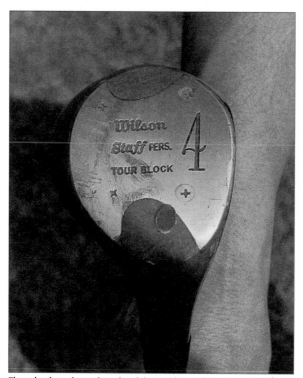

The sole plate of a modern-day club. Note how it differs from that shown on page 86. This is a No. 4 wood and is used for playing off the fairway.

But don't give up hope. There are alternatives, such as leather grips. They last for many years, but are relatively expensive and also need cleaning and refurbishing from time to time. I have recently discovered cord grips, probably the more practical of the alternatives. These grips are a little more expensive than standard ones and have a rough surface. I have not yet needed to clean mine and they give a very secure feeling, even in wet weather. But, like most things in life, nothing's perfect. They are a little harsh to delicate skin. Especially when practicing, if your hold on the club allows any movement, chafing and even blistering will quickly result. However, this is a useful teaching aid. Your grip simply isn't good enough.

For a quick check, apply the Henry Cotton test. He told me, many years ago, that a golfer with a good grip should be able to line up six balls on the practice grounds and hit them all away without re-gripping. It was a very valid point. If you need to re-grip, you've allowed the club to slip in your grasp. This is an opportunity, like it or not, to examine the way you are holding the club. Whatever your grip, strong or weak, it must not allow the club to move in the hands.

The insert is the part of the wood that makes contact with the ball. Note
the screws on this insert; you should make sure they are flush with the
plate otherwise they will damage your ball and cause irregular flight
paths after contact.

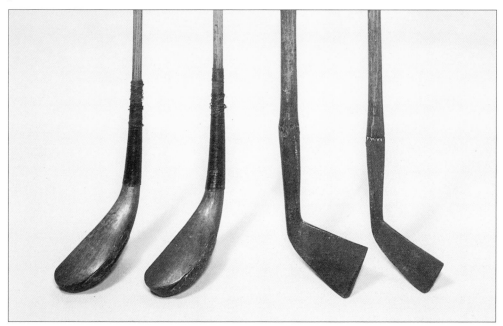

Eighteenth century woods and irons. If you look closely at the two woods
you will see that even in those days they had inserts on the faces.

# FROM THE FAIRWAY

# INTRODUCTION

The fairway, in golf, is defined as any closely-mown area 'through the green'. That is, any part of the golf course to which you are expected to hit the ball, except tees and greens.

This means a great variety of shots, using every club in the bag – including driver and putter. Length can be anything from a shot of anything up to 300 yards with a driver from a good lie, to a putt from the fringe of a green to a flag just a few yards away.

Playing from the fairway with woods and irons is equally broad in scope as far as swing speeds are concerned, and can achieve anything from a full shot to the most delicate pitch and chip.

**LEFT:** Playing from the fairway – the closely-mown area between tee and green – demands shots as varied as a full-blooded wood, a sweetly struck mid-iron and a delicate chip a few yards out from the flag.

# THE FAIRWAY WOODS

T his term is really one of the silliest in golf. Other materials have partly replaced wood – predominantely metal – but to date, no one has invented a better term. At least, everyone knows what it means.

## THE DRIVER

Yes – your driver really is a fairway wood, but how many golfers ever dream of using it except from a tee peg?

To some extent, there is wisdom in this attitude. Certainly, the driver is mostly to be used when the ball is perched up invitingly and because it is the longest club in the set, it should, in theory, be the most difficult one to use consistently. However, there are certain situations when the driver is well worth considering

### WHEN YOUR BALL IS LYING VERY WELL
In this case, the grassy lie acts as a kind of substitute for a tee peg. On some courses – certain links for example, where the fine grasses tend to grow sideways rather than upwards – you will seldom find such a lie. On others, where growth is dense, or where the strain of grass seems to support the ball, very good lies are by no means rare.

When you find one such lie, and you also need distance, the driver could be the club to use. Basically, the shot is approached in just the same way as a normal tee shot, with just one or two slight differences.

If you are an 'animal' on the tee, always striving for the big hit and not worrying too much about accuracy, then you will have to make adjustments. Your ball may be sitting up and begging for it, but it's still much easier to duff your shot than it is from a tee peg.

Just for once, subdue your animal instincts, and swing at about 80 per cent power. You can help to control the

LEFT AND BELOW: Most golfers would only think of using their driver from the tee. However, provided you have a good lie, grip the club a couple of inches lower than usual and swing smoothly at less than full power, there is nothing to stop you playing this club from the fairway. On the other hand you can use an iron from the tee.

clubhead by sacrificing a little distance and gripping the club a couple of inches lower down.

### WHEN YOU NEED TO KEEP THE BALL LOW

This can be the case in either of two situations: when an obstacle, often low branches, lies ahead of you, and when you need to keep your ball down, under the main force of a wind.

Even if your ball isn't lying ideally, you should be prepared to use your driver in these circumstances. Your club loft is unlikely to be more than 12 degrees, so the same swing as you would use with a 3 wood is mechanically certain to propel your ball along a lower trajectory.

There is, of course, a danger of half-thinning the ball if your lie is unfavorable, but even this can be an advantage: your ball is even more certain to keep low, and although it won't fly a long way, ought to get plenty of run in average or dry conditions.

### IF YOU HABITUALLY SLICE OR FADE

If you're one of these players, you won't have much difficulty in getting your ball airborne, whatever the loft of the club you're using . But you will find the extra length that your driver will give you from the fairway very useful. You know – the club isn't really as difficult as all that.

Conversely, if you hook or draw the ball, you'd probably do best to leave the driver alone, unless, that is, you are a good enough striker to feel full of confidence. The driver is always worth considering, however, if a low, running shot seems to be what the situation demands.

### IF YOU HIT DOWN WITH ALL YOUR WOODS

A driver shot from a tee peg is normally played with the clubhead travelling on the level at impact, or even slightly on the upswing. Many players, however, hit down on the ball – which isn't necessarily the mark of an inferior player.

Early in his professional career, Arnold Palmer didn't just hit down on the ball – he deliberately aimed to hit the ground first and the ball second. His club bounced into the ball, especially on hard ground.

Hitting down on the ball with a driver does reduce the length obtained from the tee. The ball is hit a slightly glancing blow, and not with a flow along the target line. There is also more backspin. The usual result is more height and less carry and run.

However, this can be turned to advantage when playing from the fairway. Such a player might be every bit as long as he would be from a tee peg.

**BELOW:** When the ball is teed-up it is fairly easy to get it airborne with a driver. Although it is harder to do this from the fairway, hitting down into the back of the ball will impart more backspin and help to give you more height.

**OPPOSITE:** For greater accuracy without loss of distance, many professionals carry a I-iron in place of a 4-wood.

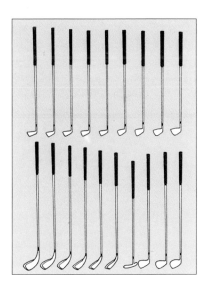

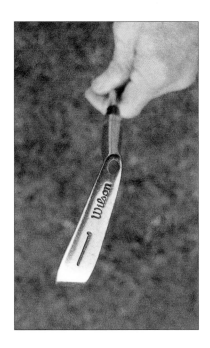

**ABOVE:** A full range of clubs from which a player can choose to make up a full set of 14. Top row – irons (1-9); Bottom row – woods (driver, 2, 3, 4 and 7), a putter, two wedges and a sand wedge.

I remember talking to Dai Rees, the great Welsh golfer, some years ago, on the subject of Henry Cotton and his length. He told me that the great triple Open Champion wasn't exceptionally long from the tee, but that he was when using his driver from the fairway.

At his best, Cotton was one of the few great players who tried to hit every shot straight (Byron Nelson is the only other example I can think of), so he didn't have the advantages which a fader does, for example. However, in his very great days, Cotton was a striker of superb precision: perhaps he didn't have to restrict his swing to maintain control when using his driver from the fairway.

### IF YOUR DRIVER HAS MORE LOFT THAN THE AVERAGE

There are no rules laid down for the amount of loft on the face of a driver – or any other club, for that matter.

For a driver, the loft can vary between 8 and 12 degrees. But club manufacturers know full well that most golfers would find an 8-degree loft difficult or even impossible. Any player, however accomplished, who draws the ball, or has his hands well forward of the clubhead at impact might well find this to be the case.

So manufacturers tend to produce far more drivers with lofts at the top end of the range. What you are getting, you might say, isn't a driver at all, but something much more like a 2-wood. You have a club which can easily get the ball airborne for you from a reasonable fairway lie.

## HOW MANY WOODS?

The rules of golf limit us to 14 clubs. It is up to each individual golfer to decide on the combination which is best.

Most players, for example, find that on any average day, they are better with woods than they are with irons – or vice versa. This gives a clear choice – is it better to try to improve a weakness or to play to one's strength?

The great Hungarian soccer player, Ferenc Puskas provides an example of one solution to this dilemma. He was said to have 'no right foot', a charge which worried the roly-poly Hungarian not in the least. He concentrated his practice on honing his skills and developing his power with the left.

You could take a leaf from the Puskas book if, for example, your strength lies in the long irons. Many tournament players make only limited use of their woods, even from the tee. If they can crack a 1-iron more than 250 yards, they might not carry a fairway wood at all. They might occasionally use a driver from the fairway, and don't miss the extra distance which a fairway wood would give them.

But these are superb strikers of the ball, with very fast hands – both essentials for consistent long hitting with a 1- iron. For the average player, the 1-iron is the most difficult club of all to use, and off-center strikes do not travel nearly as far as the same amount of error would give you when using a wood. The poor long iron player will almost certainly score better by making more use of woods.

The standard set of woods on offer at your pro shop will be driver, 3 and 4, or driver, 3 and 5, but this comes nowhere near representing the choice available.

I once played golf with a man who had no irons in his bag at all, except a blade putter. Admittedly, he was an exceptional case; a man who had been driven to give up the game, at one time, by intolerable shanking. Then a friend told him that you could buy a complete set of clubs, all of which were woods, and he was soon happily pitching away with a short-shafted wood bearing the number '10' on the sole plate, and so on, back through the set to the driver.

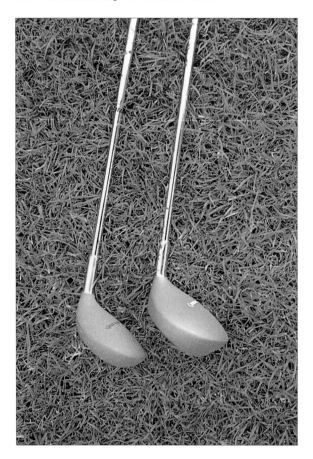

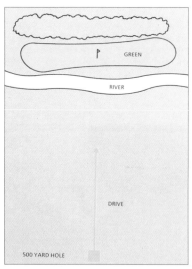

**ABOVE:** A long approach to a narrow green such as this requires a high-flighted shot if the ball is to clear the stream and stop quickly without running into the trees behind.

**LEFT:** A metal-headed driver and a 5-wood – both have their uses off the tee and on the fairway. Note the small head of the latter.

Not that I'm suggesting you do the same. My playing partner lacked precision from, say, 100 yards in. His woods gave him limited backspin, and even with his 10-wood, he sometimes hit the ball much too far – perhaps when he got his hands well ahead of the clubhead at impact, and therefore de-lofted the club.

There are, however, far less extreme options worth your consideration, which involve dropping only the long irons from your set. You might carry a driver for your tee shots, and a 3- or 4-wood for length from the fairway.

Now, we are in the area of substituting woods for irons. Let's take a look at the various uses of the 5-wood and start with an example.

One of the most dominant performances ever seen at the US Masters was the display put on by Raymond Floyd in 1976. He opened up with rounds of 65 and 66, and eventually cruised home by eight strokes; this in an event which seems to produce more close finishes and play-offs than most.

Sales of the 5-wood soared in the USA. Why?

Simply because Floyd had given considerable thought to which clubs he would carry in that year's Masters, giving close attention to how Augusta's par 5's should be played. He decided that high flight to the greens on these holes was important, because he needed, not only to hit the greens, but hold them as well. His 1-iron had to go. Instead, he chose to carry a 5-wood for the shape of shot it gave him.

**ABOVE:** A long fairway wood shot. The green is in the center.

The result was that Floyd played the 5's at Augusta just about as well as they have ever been played in competition. He was 13 under par for these holes!

Club golfers took note of this object lesson, at least for a while, and indeed, the benefits can be substantial. 5-woods give height, good length, and more important, are easy to play. The shorter shaft helps control, and the extra loft undoubtedly cuts down the effects of hook and draw spin.

It is often said that the 5-wood's main advantages become apparent from the rough, when the small head pushes easily through the grass, and the loft gets the ball airborne quickly. Neither of these factors matter in the least from the fairway.

Here, there are two major uses. You can expect greater accuracy to place a second shot exactly where you want it at a par 5, and for shots to the greens you get Ray Floyd's advantage of high flight which helps to hold the greens. This is especially useful if there are water hazards, or bunkers, close to the green and between you and the flag: you can hit over them without incurring the excessive run you'll get from a long iron.

**BELOW:** If you are coming in over this water hazard you need a high shot to clear it and hold the green beyond – a 5-wood might be the solution from some distance out.

There are other 'utility' woods which are worth considering, although you won't find them in every pro shop. As you'd expect, the most common are the 6 and 7. Depending on the swing characteristics of individual players, these two cover distances roughly equivalent to those given by 3- to 5-irons. From the fairway, their benefits are just about the same as those of the 5-wood, except, of course, for reduced length and higher flight.

# 3- AND 4-WOODS

There is so little difference in the usefulness of these two
woods that it is not worth separating them. Unlike the 4- and
5-irons, we seldom use these woods where the slight
difference in length will be significant.

Imagine you are trying to hit a far-distant green. Your
success or otherwise will be decided by the quality of your
strike, and whether you were right to select a wood in the first
place, than by which of these two woods you decided to use.

It's a bit extravagant to have both of these woods in your
bag. In any case, you will tend to use the one in which you
have more confidence. It would be better, therefore, to
discard the less-favored club and replace with with a second
pitching wedge, with more loft than your usual one.

My general advice would be to stay with a 3-wood if you
cut the ball. In that case, you need the extra length which this
club gives you, and you should have no problem getting your
shots off the ground. If you tend to draw the ball, the reverse
advice would apply. The 4-wood will work better, because you
probably tend to take some loft from the clubface, and
consequently smother a proportion of your shots.

Playing either club is just the same as using a driver
from the fairway – but easier. The shorter shafts aid control of
the clubhead, and the extra loft lessens slice or hook spin.

The smaller heads are also useful when the ball finds a
fluffy lie – a patch where the mowers haven't cut quite as
closely as elsewhere. Much the same is true when the lie is
bare of grass. In this case, although an iron might still be the
club to play, the way the clubhead of a fairway wood sits to
the ball gives more confidence than a driver head would. This
can be the constant situation on the sort of tight lies found
on links courses.

**LEFT:** A 3-wood – the
shorter shaft and
greater degree of loft
makes it easier to
play from the fairway
than a longer-shafted
and flatter-faced
driver.

**ABOVE AND RIGHT:** The address and early stages of the backswing when playing a 3-wood from a slightly fluffy lie on the fairway. Note the position of the ball in relation to the golfer's left heel. It is slightly further back in the stance than it would be if this shot were being played from a flatter lie. This helps to minimize the risk of trapping grass between the club face and ball just before impact. Note also the smooth take away and the shoulders beginning to turn.

**ABOVE AND LEFT:** At the top, the downswing and the finish. Note the full shoulder turn at the top, the return to a square position just before impact and the high finish – all indicating that the golfer has hit powerfully through the ball in an effort to ensure elevation, length and accuracy.

A 3-wood from a better lie this time, and the ball is slightly further forward in the stance.

Having checked his line the golfer addresses the ball.

A smooth take away, and no sign of the wrists breaking at this stage.

The wrists just begin to break

The wrist continue to break as the shoulders begin to turn.

The shoulders nearly at full turn as the golfer approaches the top of the backswing.

Well into the downswing now, with the wrists still cocked and the shoulders coming back to a square-on position.

Finally, through the ball with the shoulders and hips completing a full turn to ensure length and accuracy.

# THE IRONS

'Only God can hit a 1-iron.' This is one of the whole series of golfing *bon mots* invented by Lee Trevino – or, the uncharitable would suggest, his script writer – over the years. There may be some justification for it, but it has become less true over the years.

What Lee had in mind, was the fact that the 1-iron *used* to be a very difficult club to play consistently, and perhaps the most unforgiving club in the bag. Many – perhaps the majority of – tournament players preferred not to play the club, stopping short at the 2-iron, or perhaps the 3-iron, substituting an extra wood. This was even more true of club players. 20 or 30 years ago, very few carried a 1-iron.

All golfers face the same problem to some degree. In terms of lost distance, it was a very unforgiving club when the player missed the 'sweet spot', compared with the effect of an off-center shot with a wooden club. The actual distance lost from a pure or merely so-so strike with a wood is often remarkably little.

Things were quite different with a 1-iron. A poor strike seemed to get you nowhere at all, and the club found very little favor for tee shots. Lack of loft meant, and still means, that spin imparted by an inadvertent slice or hook makes the ball swing far more wildly, left or right, than is the case when the same shot is hit with, say a 4-wood.

Highly accomplished players welcome this. If you have the ability to bend the ball either way at will, the straight face of a 1-iron will enhance this skill, and improve your chances of bringing off the desired shot.

Nowadays, perimeter weighting on so many clubs has greatly reduced the terrors of the 1-iron. This type of clubhead design ensures that the off-center shot isn't punished by loss of distance to anything like the same degree. The ability to use the club no longer belongs to the Almighty alone.

In recent years, the most renowned user of the 1-iron has probably been Sandy Lyle. One of the game's most

**LEFT** The key to playing a good shot with a 1-iron is to swing smoothly. At address the ball is positioned two to three inches inside the left heel.
**RIGHT:** As you take the club back, don't be tempted to break the wrists too early.

**LEFT AND RIGHT:** The wrists should begin to break at or just before waist-height – as the shoulders begin to turn.

**LEFT:** At the top of the swing the shoulders have reached full-turn and the shaft is not quite parallel to the ground. **RIGHT AND BELOW:** Just after impact, and the player is swinging smoothly through the ball to ensure a good turn and a high finish.

powerful players, he makes little use of the driver during an average round, getting all the length he needs from his 1-iron – 260 yards plus – and he feels far more confident of keeping his ball on the fairway.

We, however, would probably do better to avoid thinking of using this club for great distance. Such a train of thought quite often leads to the use of excessive force. Better to behave as you would with a 5-iron in your hands: use a full swing, but think rhythm, balance and precision.

## THE LONG IRONS

We have considered the 1-iron separately, because, unarguably one of the long irons, it is still a specialist club. The remainder (2 through 4), entail no significant difference in the way they are played. The stance and the swing both remain unaltered.

But beware of that word 'long'. It does suggest, don't you think, that you are supposed to hit a long way with them. This often persuades golfers to lash at the ball.

**ABOVE:** The peripheral weighting incorporated into the head of this 1-iron has enlarged the sweet spot and made it more forgiving of the less-than-perfect strike.

**BELOW:** Just as you would with any other club, adopt a comfortable address position with a long iron and don't try to belt the ball a long distance.

Remember, that these irons are merely clubs designed to vary the distance the ball travels. When considering your shot, your attitude should be exactly the same as when you are playing, say, a 7-iron. Your aim is to hit a target, and you choose a club which will give you the required length. Having done that – go ahead. Use your normal swing speed, thinking precision, rather than striving for maximum distance.

It will do no harm at all if you can maintain the same attitude as when you are playing a full pitch. Although you should swing at high speed, about 20 per cent of your capacity should remain unused.

**RIGHT:** Having selected the long iron, line up square to the target and make sure you aren't standing too close to the ball.

**RIGHT:** Take the club back square to, and as the shoulders turn, inside the line.

**RIGHT:** At the top of the swing the club should be pointing towards the target.

**RIGHT:** Pull the club back down inside the line, with the shoulders returning to a square-on position.

**RIGHT:** Let the momentum of the swing uncock the wrists,

**RIGHT:** . . . and at impact drive smoothly through with the right arm and shoulder – but don't force the shot.

**RIGHT:** Turn the shoulders and hips and produce a high finish.

Again, a comfortable address position.

A smooth, one-piece take away.

Wrists break and shoulders begin to turn.

Back nearly square-on to the target.

Club slightly over the parallel this time.

Keeping inside the line and not stretching for the ball.

Accelerating into impact.

Driving legs, hand, arms and shoulders through the ball. . .

to produce a full turn and a high finish.

# THE MID-IRONS

As the term implies, these are clubs around the middle of the range; the 5-, 6- and 7-irons. Many club professionals, giving lessons to beginners, start their pupils off using one of these clubs. They are the easiest to use, the shafts are not long (which helps), and lofts are not extreme in either direction. Pupils, it is hoped, won't be discouraged by hitting a series of unsuccessful shots.

Mid-irons should be played with a square stance, and a ball position approximately inside the left heel. The only difference from swinging a long iron is that the shorter shafts lead to a more upright swing plane.

You may well find that one of these clubs – the 6-iron is probably the most likely candidate – becomes the one in which you have the most confidence from your whole set. If this proves to be the case, you can capitalize by making extra use of it.

The 6-iron, for example, gives quite good length, and can be used for this purpose for second shots on a par 5 from poor fairway lies, or when the ball isn't sitting up in the semi-rough. Used well below full power, the club can also be useful for pitching, particularly to soft, holding greens.

Here the player has to clear some trees and a bunker to reach the green.

A mid-iron will give him the necessary loft, and a smooth, one-piece take away gives him a good start.

Because of the shorter shaft length, the wrists will break slightly earlier with a mid-iron than a long iron.

The player could have stopped here before beginning his downswing . . .

but he went just over the parallel.

A good position as the club head returns to the ball.

At impact.

Well through the ball now.

And a good finish, with the hands above
head height.

Playing a 6-iron from the fairway.

The 6-iron is one of the most versatile and easiest of clubs to play.

**ABOVE:** A mid-iron this time, but you should adopt the same approach as for a long iron – although the shorter shaft length will mean that you will be standing slightly shorter and a bit closer to the ball.

**ABOVE RIGHT:** Again, note the one-piece take away – the left arm straight and the wrists unbroken.

**LEFT:** Although the overall position is good at the top of the swing, the club has gone over the parallel. This can lead to a loss of control on the downswing and shouldn't be necessary with a mid-iron.

**RIGHT:** Again, this is a position as the swing nears completion. The head, shoulders, chest and hips have been driven almost square to the target by the fluid momentum of the swing.

**RIGHT:** The right heel high off the ground, high hands and the club around the back of the neck mark the finish of a full and well-struck mid-iron.

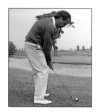

# THE SHORT PITCH

T oday, the word 'chip' is quite often used to refer to what I, and many others, would call a 'pitch'. This is particularly true when the shot in question is, in fact, a short pitch, so perhaps I'd better define my terms.

The short pitch is, quite simply, a shot that the golfer visualizes, and hopes to play, mainly through the air. Even over very short distances, it will rise quite high, and has little run.

**RIGHT:** A poor pitch from here and you would end up in the water hazard!

Just off the green and a chip with a short iron . . .

. . . gets the ball into the air and onto the putting surface.

With humpy ground between you and the green . . .

. . . you must pitch over it to get to the flag.

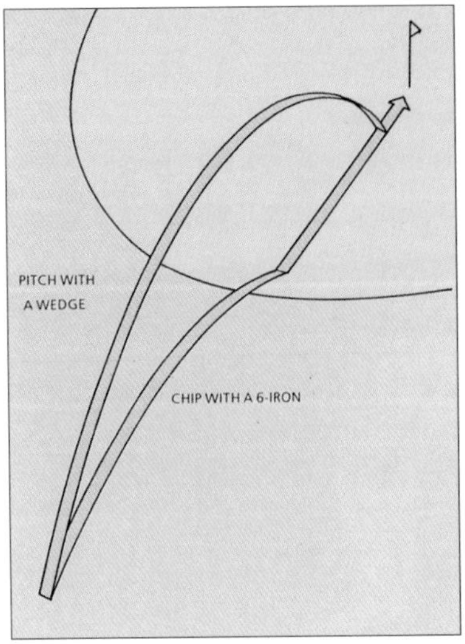


**ABOVE:** From the same position off the green, a pitch with a wedge will have a higher trajectory. and will land closer to the flag and stop quicker than an equivalent chip with a 6-iron.

In this sense, a short pitch may be played only a few yards from the flag – over a greenside bunker, perhaps, to a flag set close by. If you played a chip, which is a low, running shot, you'd finish in the sand under your nose, or run on well past the flag.

Though this is a situation where a cut-up shot has to be played, the necessity for taking that sort of risk rapidly decreases when the flag isn't quite as close. Now, we are in the territory of the short pitch.

This is played in a straightforward manner, without any need to open the face and cut across the line of flight.

But it still isn't simple, perhaps because many golfers are uncomfortable when employing a half or three-quarter swing. There are two pitfalls to avoid:

(1) Don't take a short backswing, and then push your hands into the shot, at the last moment, to make up for the loss of pace which your too-short backswing has landed you with.

(2) If your backswing *is* long enough – even too long, perhaps – don't decelerate into the ball.

As you can see, these are opposite hazards, and they indicate that a major difficulty of the very short pitch is feel and control of length, pace and rhythm of your swing.

Set up with your shoulders parallel to the target line, and with the ball, either opposite the left heel, or just slightly further back in your stance. For a start, play with your feet parallel, too, but you may, after practice, find it easier to play with your left foot a couple of inches withdrawn. This gives more freedom to swing hands and arms through, but if you find you're cutting across the ball, then you should revert to a wholly square stance.

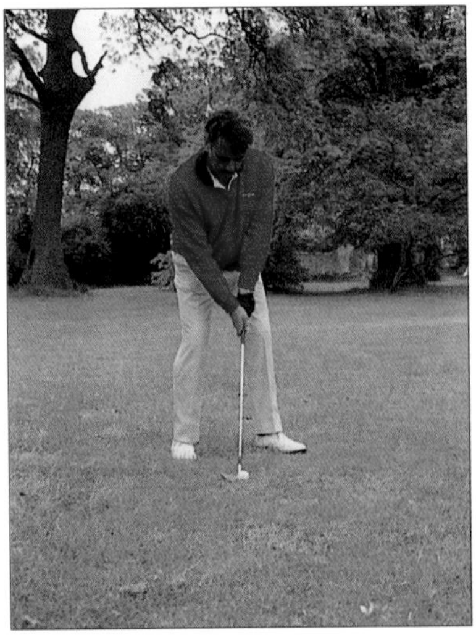

**RIGHT:** A slightly open stance for a short pitch.

Setting up for a full pitch.

Feet square to the line and the ball inside the left heel.

Take the club back smoothly – don't 'pick it up' with the hands.

Shoulder beginning to turn.

A three-quarter swing takes you to the top.

Halfway down and the shoulders are squaring up again.

The momentum of the swing gives
you a high finish.

Assessing the results.

To clear this bunker and get the ball close to the flag . . .

. . . all that's needed is a short, firm swing (not a jab) . . .

In this shot, exact striking means a great deal, in terms of both distance and trajectory. Help yourself to achieve this by gripping down towards the bottom of the handle.

The length of your backswing will depend on the distance required, and the club you have selected. But remember – it should never be very short, because that would invariably lead to a jab rather than a swinging movement. Not less than waist high, and not often much more than shoulder height are useful rules of thumb.

Think of the shot as one played by arms and shoulders, with the wrists only breaking on rather longer pitch shots. Otherwise, the hands should be kept out of this shot as much as possible. This way, you eliminate the danger of letting the clubhead get ahead of the hands which is one of the prime causes of inconsistency.

. . . to produce a near-perfect result.

129

As with long and mid-irons, a full pitch to a green, demands . . . . . . a smooth, one-piece take away . . .

. . . a full turn of the shoulders . . .

. . . taking the club to either just short of parallel to the ground . . .

... or parallel – and on line with the target ...

... before bringing it back down inside the line ...

... and hitting through the ball ...

... to a high finish.

Don't be tempted to lift your head early ...

... or you'll top it into the trees.

A typical shot from the fairway.

When you are in good form, you may just be able to get away with this, but you won't succeed week-in and week-out.

Visualize what happens when the clubhead does get ahead of the hand. The amount by which this occurs is certain to vary. The loft of your club effectively changes, the amount of height achieve varies, and it becomes quite impossible to be consistent

The shorter the pitch shot, the more useful it is to use your putting grip. This is especially true if you keep your wrists out of your putting stroke. Let me give you an example: like many other great players, Jack Nicklaus has been accused of being 'finished' at various times in his career. Curtis Strange, Tom Watson, Sandy Lyle and Seve Ballesteros had the same accusation levelled at them in the 1990 season. Hale Irwin was definitely thought of as a figure of the past – until he won the 1990 US Open. We just never know, until we have the advantage of the perspective of history.

Jack Nicklaus first faced this judgement towards the end of the 1960s. He had been enormously successful, but his record began to decline in major championships. The talking stopped when he won the 1970 British Open.

All went well until 1979, when Jack had a bad year in all kinds of competition. By now, he was on the verge of his 40th birthday, so perhaps there was more justification for supposing his career at the top was over. Although he had lost some length, he felt that his major weakness was in his short game, which had never been a strong feature. His putting, however, had always been very good indeed.

Jack then took on short-game expert, Phil Rodgers, as coach, principally to improve the range and precision of his shots around the green. Rodgers taught him a lot, and suggested, among other things, that he use his conventional reverse overlap putting grip for short pitching and chipping.

In 1980, Nicklaus became one of the few men to win two majors in a year – the US Open and US PGA.

I don't suggest, for a moment, that this technique will revolutionize your game, but it could help you to feel that the short pitch is a shot played with arms and shoulders, rather than with a wristy flick.

Many beginners, and even advanced, players feel that the short pitch shot is the weakest part of their game. The two prime reasons for this are the necessity for exact length and for very good, consistent striking. The angle of loft of the pitching club must remain constant if an identical result from the same swing speed is to be achieved. It is worth persistent practice to ensure that the hands are always ahead of the clubhead at impact, and that the *amount* by which they are ahead is constant.

When this varies, you are, in effect, using the angle of loft of, say, a wedge for one shot, followed by an 8- or perhaps

**RIGHT:** The results of two fine pitches to the green.

If you have a good lie . . .

. . . a short pitch with a sand wedge . . .

. . . will give you more height than with a
pitching wedge . . .

. . . and allow you to stop the ball quickly on
the green.

a sand iron next time. No one can possibly be a consistent short pitcher if they are 'flippy wristed'.

As with long putting, distance is more important than direction when pitching. Imagine that your ball has been pitched three yards too far. The difference is negligible if your shot was directly over the flag or was a yard or two either side However, it certainly matters if you are always getting your distance right, but are consistently wide of the hole.

To improve your direction, take just as much care when setting up to square your clubface along the target line as you would if you were putting. Many tend to let nature do the job for them, but that's usually not good enough. If your hand position is consistent, that should do the job for you.

For a very short pitch, open the blade of the club to the line of the shot . . .

## CLUB SELECTION FOR THE SHORT PITCH

Although the short pich is, by definition, a short shot, there is still a range of possibilities when selecting a club. The sand iron is probably the most effective choice from good lies, because a ball which stops quickly from such a gentle strike will do so because of its height, not from backspin. However, the extreme loft of the club makes it a little more difficult to achieve consistency. Most people will probably find that the wedge will give a better average result.

When you have sufficient green to play with, a 9-iron, or perhaps the 8-iron can be used. They are easier clubs with which to achieve consistent distance through the air, and it's easy to learn to adjust for the greater run which results from the less extreme lofts.

. . . minimize wrist movement during the short backswing. . .

## THE MEDIUM PITCH

Here, we are talking about marginal differences. The short pitch is played with a mini-swing, while the medium pitch simply means you take a longer swing – about three-quarters – while making your strike considerably firmer.

As the medium pitch needs far less feel, it is, hopefully, easier to play. Penalties for an imprecise strike are less severe, because we don't really expect to lay this shot dead by the side of the hole.

. . . and hit firmly through the ball.

## THE FULL PITCH

So far, I've not mentioned distance, and said very little about club selection. These omissions are deliberate: all pitches are simply shots which travel along a high trajectory, and run

**LEFT TO RIGHT, TOP TO BOTTOM:** For a medium length pitch again, make a one-piece take away and don't take more than a three-quarter length swing. Strike the ball firmly all the while concentrating on the length of the shot.

Take a full backswing for a full-length pitch.

From top to bottom, the different trajectories of a sand wedge, a wedge, a 9-iron, an 8-iron and a 5-iron.

along the ground for a relatively short distance. It therefore doesn't matter what number is inscribed on your club. Trajectory and run are what counts.

But there are limits. A searing 1-iron which seriously incommodes a butterfly alighting on a buttercup is obviously no pitch. We might well draw a line at a club with the maximum loft of a 5-iron, and then only if the player naturally gets a high flight from his shots.

Normally, we think of the pitching clubs as 8- through sand iron, as the up-and-down flight of the pitch shades into a more shallow arc, roughly from this point.

Whatever the club, however, the full pitch remains basically the same shot, but played with a full swing of the club. But do remember that it is a precision shot, and that your swing should always be under complete control. Keep a measured pace, and never lash at the ball. Try to ignore the golfer who delights in hitting his pitching clubs the maximum distance he can wring out of them, and then crows about getting 'up with a drive and a 9-iron . There are no prizes for how far you hit a pitch. What counts is how close you get to the hole.

To help you remember this, and also to assist your control, grip one or two inches down the shaft.

Addressing the ball with an 8-iron.

As with the other irons, making a one-piece take away.

Nearing the top of the swing.

At the top of the swing for a full 8-iron shot.

Swinging through the ball.

Once again, to a high finish.

**LEFT:** Addressing the ball with a pitching wedge.

**RIGHT:** Wrist beginning to break after a one-piece take away.

**LEFT:** At the top of the swing for a full shot.

**RIGHT:** Hitting firmly through the ball.

**LEFT:** Nearing the top of the swing.

**RIGHT:** A full turn, and the ball's on its way to the flag.

## THE LOW SAND IRON (WEDGE)

The most remarkable golfer to emerge immediately following World War II was Bobby Locke. His technique in the long game was highly unorthodox: he had a great loop in his backswing, went right out of plane at the top of it, and his left wrist was anything but firm. But he had great feel for his swing, and found the fairway very consistently.

His legendary strengths were in his short game. Locke's putting was a source of wonder, and his abilities with the short irons were superb. Again, his feel for his swing and judgement of distance seemed to guarantee that, even if he was occasionally a little off line, he was invariably pin high.

One of his specialities was the use of the low-flying wedge, which he played with a broad-soled club of his own design, broadly similar to a conventional sand iron, with the mass of clubhead weight right at the sole.

In contrast, today's conventional wedge is often far more similar to a 9-iron with extra loft. In other words, it's a 10-iron, and is sometimes numbered as such.

Playing this club demands a change in your usual set up. The ball is positioned approximately opposite your right heel,

and the toe of the club is turned in. This is to compensate for the tendency of the blade to open at address, owing to the ball's position, so unusually far back in your stance.

The hands should fall naturally into position, well ahead of your clubhead, which is precisely where you want them to be, at address and impact. The backswing should be comparatively short, perhaps not much more than waist high, and the wrists should be kept firm throughout. However, it is important to avoid too short a backswing.

The action into the ball is very much a pull, with no wrist movement whatsoever. You should have the feeling that you are pulling the ball towards the flag, rather than striking it towards the target.

Your swing will be very much down at the ball, on a steep arc, producing extreme backspin, with the ball being squeezed between clubhead and turf.

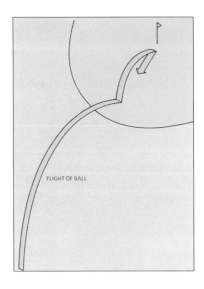

**ABOVE:** The considerable backspin imparted by a low-flying wedge shot takes effect on the second bounce of the ball, and will bring it to an abrupt halt or, on some occasions, roll it back towards you.

**BELOW:** When your ball is up against a collar of rough, thinning it with the leading edge of a wedge will get you out of trouble.

There are various advantages to this shot, not least the benefits you will obtain in strong winds. Whatever the wind direction, the effect on the ball will be minimal, because the low flight of the ball keeps it well below the wind's main strength. When playing into a gale, a high pitch shot simply can't be judged: your ball may even be blown back towards you. If the wind is behind you, much backspin is taken off once it gets up into the air.

Of course, there will still be some effect from the wind, just as there is when playing the putt, which is the lowest shot of all, but it will be minimized, and more experience will enable you to make allowances much more easily than you can for high shots.

One thing you'll relish is that this shot, well played, is spectacular. Low flight, combined with speed through the air, makes it seem certain that your ball will finish many yards beyond the hole. The first bounce does nothing at all to change that impression. But when the ball makes contact with the ground for the second time, the extreme backspin really takes effect, and the ball stops dead – perhaps even spins back towards you.

Other advantages of the shot include the extra confidence it will give you when playing from a bare lie. Unless your sand iron has a very low trailing edge, that advanced hand position will make you feel very confident of good ball contact.

It's quite possible to make this shot your standard method on short approach, but there are drawbacks to it. When greens are variable it doesn't work at all consistently. Remember that the professionals you see in tournaments derive remarkable backspin because the greens they are playing on are in peak condition. However closely they are cut, and however fast they putt, grass growth is very dense, which greatly helps the ball's backspin to grip the putting surface.

You won't get consistent results when this isn't so. Neither will you when greens through a round of golf vary from soft to firm.

## THE THINNED WEDGE

Golfers afflicted with problems on the greens have used just about every club in the bag, with the exception of the lofted irons, for putting. My 'thinned wedge' is really a specialized kind of putt

Quite often, during a golfing year, your ball will come to rest just off the green, resting either against the beginning of the fringe of the green, or a little further on – on the fringe and against longer grass beyond. Whether you decide to chip or putt, the problem is the same – even though you may bring your club quite steeply down on the ball, blades of grass will intrude.

This is where our thinned wedge comes in. Address the ball with the leading edge of your club aligned against the equator of the ball. Your gentle strike should not be impeded by grass, but it must still be precise. If you make contact just below the equator, your ball will hop, rather than run, and you won't get the distance you anticipated. If contact is made much above the equator, you have a topped shot and, again, less distance.

An exact strike will give you a running ball like a putt, but beware – this shot *must* be practiced. You will have no confidence at all if you suddenly try to use it in a competitive situation, with no previous experience.

## THE CUT-UP SHOT

Often known as the 'lob', this is a difficult shot, and should only be used by golfers of average ability when full of confidence, or perhaps as an all-or-nothing shot in matchplay.

The aim of the shot, played with a sand iron or wedge, is to put maximum height on a very short pitch, so that there will be little forward momentum on the ball when it pitches on the green. Height, as well as backspin, often decides how much run there will be on the ball.

It is most useful when playing to a green on a higher level than you are, or when playing over an obstacle – a bunker perhaps – when the flag is close beyond it.

Set up with an open stance, with the ball opposite your left instep. With your body aligned to the left of your target, aim the club face at the hole, or a little left, if you expect some side spin. Lift the club sharply, as though for a bunker shot, and then swing across the target line, getting the feeling of sliding your club under the ball.

This shot is easiest to play when your ball is on a slight upslope, or is, at least, cushioned by a layer of grass on the flat.

Don't attempt to play it when you have:
(1)   A downhill lie.
(2)   A bare, or hardpan, lie.
(3)   Not practiced the shot.
(4)   No confidence in your ability to play it.

A lot can go wrong with this shot. I've seen Tom Watson, one of the masters of the lob, shank when he brought the heel of the club in first. However, a more likely fault is inexactness in sliding your clubhead into the ball. The result is likely to be a thinned shot, treating you to the sight of your ball scuttling

**ABOVE:** A cut-up shot will get the ball up into the air very quickly and land it on the green with little forward momentum.

**BELOW:** Cutting across the ball results in a high trajectory, and imparts backspin and sidespin – both of which take effect when the ball lands on the green.

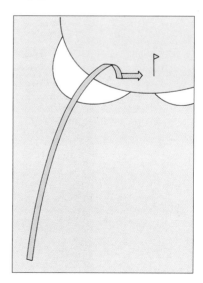

RIGHT AND FAR RIGHT:
Here we see the cut-up
shot applied to good
effect.

through the green, rather than landing, as Lee Trevino puts it, as lightly as 'a butterfly with sore feet.

Elsewhere, I have remarked that a sand iron should have a trailing edge lower than its leading edge. If you have one do not attempt to use it for the cut up shot, unless the lie is well grassed. That trailing edge is likely to catch the ground first, resulting in a bounce and the leading edge thinning the ball. Stick to your wedge. The more lofted, the better.

Although you don't need a full backswing, this should be a flowing shot, with swing energy expended in hitting the ball upward, rather than forward. Very precise contact is needed, because the club moves sharply across the ball. But when it comes off – it's a delight.

## WHY NOT THREE WEDGES?

Tom Kite is 5 feet 8 inches tall, and although 'mighty atoms' such as Ian Woosnam tend to disprove the rule, lack of height tends to mean short driving. Indeed Tom Kite is, by today's standards, by no means a long hitter, but he's among the most prolific of all money winners. Only his repeated failures to win major tournaments tarnish his reputation, and deny him his ranking among the greatest players.

Length from the tee is vital for Tour players, mainly because of the advantages which follow for playing the shot to the green. Just like club players, they are more accurate with short irons than long. This has given Kite an inbuilt disadvantage when compared with his fellow competitors when playing long 4's and par 5's. One way he can redress the balance is through his putting and his short game.

Early in the 1980s, Kite decided to abandon his 2-iron. To compensate for this at one end of the iron range, he had the lofts of his 3-, 4- and 5- changed, to fill in the gaps partially. Now he was free to carry three wedges – a sand iron, a 'strong' wedge and a 'weak' one.

This is a thought I commend to club golfers. Many of us are far more comfortable playing either full shots or little ones, but far less happy with anything in between. By this, I mean something of the order of half swing power.

Perhaps, to some extent, Tom felt the same. His strong and weak wedges gave him the opportunity to play relatively full shots with his three wedges, rather than have to play so many half power shots. He had a great money-winning year immediately afterwards, and many more since.

Golfers weren't restricted to 14 clubs until the late 1930s. In any case, in earlier years, no one even thought of carrying such a vast quantity. Open Champions around the turn of the century regarded 7 to 10 clubs as the norm. Between the wars, all this changed dramatically.

Rightly or wrongly, top professionals decided that it is far more difficult to be consistent when you have to vary your swing pace, and alter your clubface position at impact by manipulating it with the hands. They felt it was far easier to repeat a standard full swing. Some of them began to carry, not 14 clubs, but quantities soaring into the 20's.

Lawson Little, still the only player to win the Amateur Championships of both Britain and the USA in two consecutive years, was known for carrying a positive battery of pitching clubs. He would smash the ball vast distances from the tee, and then select a suitable club for 60, 85, 100 yards, and so on. Craig Wood was another power player with much the same approach. So was Walter Hagen, strange though it may seem for a player who relied on touch, rather than power.

Hagen's motives were different. He didn't actually carry his 25 clubs to use, but because he was paid a fee by a manufacturer which varied according to the number of clubs he carried. Being a logical thinker, Hagen stuffed his bag full of clubs, and held out his hand for the cheque.

We live in different times now. You could say that a full set of clubs to include most of the standard ones is 16 – four woods, 11 irons and a putter. It is up to the golfer to decide which are the most useful.

Many consider a couple of woods to be enough for their needs, and that the 1- and 2-irons are too difficult to use anyway. If you think this way, then you have already knocked four clubs out of that standard manufactured set of 16.

You already have one wedge and a sand iron, so you have room, under the Rules of Golf, not for one extra wedge but *two*.

Give it a thought.

# THE BASIC CHIP SHOT

Y ou'll sometimes hear a fellow golfer say, 'I chipped in from 100 yards.' All that proves is that he doesn't understand golf language.

I'll start by making the definitions of these terms quite clear, and by describing the differences between a chip and a pitch – which is what your fellow golfer must have been talking about.

A good chip and it's nearly stone dead.

LEFT: From this position you can either play a pitch or a chip.

RIGHT: The golfer addresses his ball . . .

LEFT: and takes the club back.

RIGHT: The ball rapidly gains height, revealing this to be a pitch and not a chip.

LEFT: The ball pitches on the playing surface . . .

RIGHT: . . . and runs up to the flag.

The differences are simple enough. The pitch travels mainly through the air, usually running for quite a short proportion of its total distance. The chip, on the other hand, is really a close relative of the putt. You should see it as a shot which mainly runs towards the flag, only the first part of its journey being through the air.

The shot is usually played from not more than a few yards of the putting surface, the basic idea being that the second or two of flight is enough to carry the ball to the putting surface. It then runs the rest of the way to the flag. Once you are further away from the green, and using more swing speed, the shot becomes more like a pitch. It will fly further through the air, because of the loft of the club, and greater momentum will impart more backspin and cause the ball to fly. It's really something halfway between a pitch and a chip. You could call it a running pitch.

The chip shot can be played with any iron in the bag, although anything more straight-faced than a 4-iron is seldom used. It's a specialized stroke, so it's wise to emulate the professionals and use very few of your clubs. In this way, you can become more accustomed to the feel of the clubs, and the way the ball responds in this very gentle stroke.

Some professionals prefer to hone their skills with just one chipping club. This probably would be a wedge, but possibly could be a 9- or sand iron.

As these are the most lofted clubs in the bag, it may be a puzzle as to why the ball runs rather than climbs into the air. The answer is that this is a gentle shot, which means that there is little backspin to persuade the ball to climb.

Far more important are the various techniques used for playing the shot. There are similarities with the putt, one important one being that there is little or no use of the wrists.

You get the feeling that you are swinging the arms back and through, getting your pace from this mini-swing, not from use of hands and wrists. You will find that, if you allow the wrists to flex, the ball will usually climb, and that your strike will become less consistent.

The length of shot determines how far you should take the club back, so there can be no firm rule about it. However, you are not flexing the wrists, so the backswing should be longer than you might at first think. Watch the professionals. Even when playing from just off the green, with the flag just a few yards away, the swing is by no means restricted to just a few inches: indeed, it looks capable of sending the ball a good many yards.

It doesn't, because they have taken the hands out of the stroke, and swing gently, though still firmly. But beware of swinging too far, and then decelerating into the ball. As with any shot, even when tapping the ball into the hole from two inches, the strike must be decisive.

**ABOVE:** Playing out under the branches of the trees calls for a long-running chip shot.

**BELOW:** The different trajectories of a chip shot played with a wedge, 8-iron, 6-iron and 4-iron.

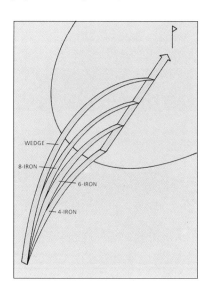

**OPPOSITE (TOP TO BOTTOM):** In this situation you could play a wedge, a 4-iron or a putter.

# STANCE

This isn't a full swing shot, so it helps to have the hips out of the way before you start, allowing your arms to swing through much more freely. Do this by taking up a slightly open stance.

Many players like to grip the club fairly well down, making the length of the club closer to that of a putter, and also enabling them to strike down a little more firmly – the longer the shaft, the longer the potential shot.

A shorter grip means that the ball will be lying closer to the feet, creating a situation closer to a putt, and getting your eyes more nearly over the ball.

So the ball is fairly close to the line of your feet, but you now have to decide how far forward or back in your stance it ought to be. The extremes are from inside the left heel to inside the right. Any further can lead to problems: too far forward and you may hit on the upswing, too far back and the swing down becomes too steep.

But there can be no firm rule, because much depends on the position of the hands.

**ABOVE:** A long chip with a 6-iron.

**ABOVE :** Gripping down the shaft of the 6-iron helps to develop a greater feel for distance.

## HANDS

The hands must be set so that they are in front of the clubhead when it meets the ball. This means that they should reach the same position as they were in the set-up – remember, you won't be flexing those wrists.

At least, you'd better not be doing anything of the sort, because if you do, you'll have no chance of an unvarying strike. The change of the blade's loft, and the height on the blade at impact will change from chip to chip. Exact striking is even more critical here than it is in putting, and a variable hand position will dramatically change the distance your chip shots travel. Lack of consistency in this part of your stroke will also lead to chips being struck fat or thin.

Making an arms-only chipping stroke obviously removes the hands from the shot. However, they do much more than simply hold the club. It can be useful to encourage one of two feelings: either that the back of the left hand is making the stroke, or that you are bowling the ball along the ground towards the hole with your right.

There's no logical reason for it, but the left hand image usually produces a lower flight and a longer run. On the other hand, thinking of the right hand can give more feel. In either case, hold on to the feeling that the face of the club is square with the back of the left hand, or the palm of the right.

But we are aiming to take the hands out of the shot altogether, so it's equally valid not to think of the hands at all. Feel the shot through upper arms or forearms – whichever you prefer.

The golfer sets
himself up for the
chip . . .

. . . makes a good take
away . . .

. . . strikes the ball . . .

. . . but wasn't firm
enough, and the ball
finishes short – never
up, never in!

# GRIP

As we have already seen elsewhere, in 1979 Jack Nicklaus suffered the first real slump of his career. After a remarkable competitive career that had already stretched for 20 years, to many it seemed likely that he had, at long last, reached the end of the road.

Jack Nicklaus didn't think so. He analyzed what had been happening to his game, and decided that his greatest playing weakness – his short game, little chips and pitches from close to the green – had deteriorated further.

So he went back to school and emerged with a great repertoire of short game strokes, as well as some changes of method.

One of the most noticeable of these was the change in his grip for chip shots. He began to use his reverse overlap putting grip.

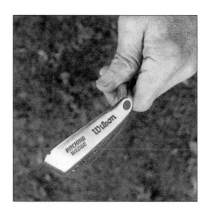
You can chip with a wedge . . .

That can be an incentive for anyone to give their putting grip a try when playing a chip. This is particularly true if you regard yourself as a good putter: it makes sense to stretch your strength on the greens a little further.

But there is one thing to watch out for. It's all too easy to become greedy, and having had some success with your putting grip, to use it further and further away from the green. If you remember that the reverse overlap grip isn't suitable for shots in which the wrists flex, you'll see that it won't work except for quite short shots.

The other grip is simplicity itself: simply chip with your normal grip for full shots. Only experiment and practice will teach you which of these two solutions is most likely to work for you.

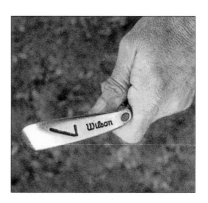
. . . a 7-iron . . .

# WEIGHT DISTRIBUTION

Set your weight a little more on the front foot than on the rear. This helps you make a slightly downward strike at the ball, and even more important, it helps you to avoid a fatal upward flick.

# CHIPPING FROM SAND

Provided that there is only a low lip facing you, a chip shot can work better than the standard splash shot, and this is particularly true when the sand is wet. However, this does need nerve: if you take any sand at all with the ball, you are left looking rather silly, because it will only have moved a couple of feet.

. . . or a 5-iron.

# CHOICE OF CLUBS

Basically, use the clubs you feel most confident with. If you are a player who prefers to use just a single club, say a wedge, for all kinds of chip shots, you will probably be playing with your hands well ahead of the clubhead. In that case, you've taken much loft from your club, reducing it to about the loft of a 7-iron from your normal stance.

Hand position alone can be used to change the flight the club puts on the ball. Opening the blade a little gives more loft, while the opposite will happen if you hood the face. Bobby Locke preferred to confine himself to one club for chips, but by making the kind of changes just described, he could make the ball react in many different ways.

The average player won't be able to produce that range. As a result, he will benefit from letting the loft of his club vary his chipping. However, if he's going to keep his feel, it's best not to use more than three clubs.

A suitable range would be a 6-iron, an 8-iron and a wedge or sand iron. Use the 6-iron when the ball is close to the putting surface, but the flag far away, producing very little backspin and minimizing the chances of the ball gripping the turf and coming to rest earlier than you would wish. Then, use the other two clubs for progressively shorter chip shots.

Some golfers would chip from here, whilst others would putt if they are less skilled at the chip shot.

# PUTT, DON'T CHIP

This may seem a negative note to end on, but it is just one way to help you make the most of your strengths.

Many club golfers think it's 'not a golf shot' to putt from more than a very few yards from the putting surface, but the pros don't think that way. They play the shots that get them the best results.

The reason that you seldom see them putting from well short of the green is that very few of them don't have great skills at chipping and short pitching. The few that don't *will* putt from many yards off, and even the others will do so occasionally, when they think they'll get a better result by putting.

A club golfer simply doesn't have that level of skills. So, if you're a good putter, but no better than average at chipping, then why not make the most of your strength? You'll be surprised at how much you can improve with more experience when putting from off the green.

You'll learn more about pace from long range, and how the ball runs over bare and rough ground. And there's one age-old truism to bear in mind: A poor putt always gets closer to the hole than a poor chip.

This golfer has decided to putt rather than chip. The ball is on its way . . .

. . . and nears the edge of the green without being deflected . . . . . . hits the upslope . . .

. . . and slows rapidly. It was worth a try with the putter from there.

# HITTING
# IT HIGH
# AND LOW

I was standing close to an oak tree, one day in 1990, working as a photographer at a tournament, some 40 yards short of a short par 4, reachable that day with a very good drive. A ball cracked into that tree, and came to rest.

This left a shot which demanded that the player thread his way close by the tree trunk, beneath low branches, negotiate a gap between the tree and a greenside bunker, and hopefully, find his way to the flag beyond.

**RIGHT:** A low chip and run is the only way out of here.

ABOVE: The green is beyond and left of centre of the big tree – a full wedge should get you there.

'Ah!' said knowledgeable father to his son, 'he'll run this one along the ground with his 5-iron.'

It seemed like a reasonable judgement. The player would have to play with touch and accuracy, and also keep his ball below the overhanging branches of the mighty oak. Then Bernhard Langer arrived. 'Sand iron', he requested caddie Peter Coleman. Was he about to waft it high over the obstacle presented by the branches? Couldn't be. They were too close.

Closer now, and a three-quarter shot with a wedge would do it.

## LOW SHOTS

Langer had elected to play a low, running shot, using a sand iron rather than a 5-iron. The probable reason for this strange-seeming choice was that, like many professionals, Langer can use his sand iron to play all manner of shots. This time, he'd be keeping his hands well ahead of the clubhead to reduce the loft of the club greatly.

He swung. But his hand position wasn't what he had intended. The ball rose too high, cracked into the tree again, and came to rest only a little further forward. It was a shot wasted; Langer hadn't taken enough loft from the clubhead, and the trajectory of his shot had been much too high.

On many inland courses, trees are one of the main problems which have to be faced and dealt with. When we get out of position, through the green, they come between us and the target, so that we have to get over them, under the lower branches, or sometimes attempt to get through a gap, perhaps halfway up – very difficult, because the shot requires subtle, not extreme, variation in trajectory.

One of the easiest ways to play a low shot is to let the loft of the club do the work for you. For example, you may be a

Closer still – a cut-up shot might be called for.

Even closer, and you might have to chip under the branches from this range.

full 9-iron distance from the flag, but the loft of the club would have you clattering into that infernal tree. Instead, depending on the height of the branches, you need to choose a much straighter-faced club.

You may, perhaps, judge that you need the loft of a 3-iron, because you need very low flight. Go ahead and try it, but it's by no means easy, because you have to judge the pace of your swing (perhaps about quarter-power) and then how the ball will run. In our earlier example, Bernhard Langer almost certainly played his unsuccessful sand iron because he was confident about how the ball would behave.

A quite different approach to keeping the ball low under branches is to hood the face of your club. Set up with the ball well back in your stance, hands well ahead of the clubhead. By doing these things, you've changed the loft of, say, an 8-iron to something much closer to a 3-iron, played with a normal stance.

Swing with little or no wrist break, and keep the feeling of maintaining the hands ahead of the clubhead, while pulling through the ball. You will find the shot easier to accomplish if you also grip down the shaft.

The foregoing applies only to quite short shots, but there's no real difference for longer shots except that it isn't possible to play full swing shots with the ball set far back in your stance. All the other principles apply.

All this only applies where the grass is closely mown. Once the grass is long, you are confronted by the chance that your low shot might be killed by the long grass before it is properly airborne. In that case, you have to visualize your shot, and go for the best compromise; one which will give you the best prospect of clearing clinging grass, while also keeping below the obstacle.

From this distance you can either go over the top or underneath.

Here the branches are overhanging the player. However, the ball won't rise quickly enough to cause problems.

When the hands are well ahead of the ball, the clubface is hooded. Note the reduced loft of this 9-iron.

For longer shots, where maximum distance is needed, higher swing speeds mean that your ball is far more likely to rise quickly because of greater backspin. Therefore, it follows that the clubs with the least loft will work best – the driver and longest irons.

Continue to play the shot with the feeling that you are pulling the clubhead through the ball, gripping down the handle of the club, and keeping the hands ahead. Swing well within yourself, remembering that keeping the ball low is of paramount importance.

A low runner of 180 yards is a lot more rewarding than contact with those low branches.

**ABOVE:** The upslope will help the player to gain height on the shot.

**LEFT:** Not a shot for the faint-hearted!

# HIGH SHOTS

Let's take that Langer oak as an example. It was near a green, and the first decision was which particular route to take?

One option, of course, is the 'low road'. Another, is to accept the likely – but not certain – loss of a shot by playing wide of the obstacle, not at the flag itself, but, perhaps, to the front or rear of the green, or perhaps a little short or long.

Or you can opt for the air route. But, if you do, you need first to be familiar with the trajectory you normally get from particular clubs, and then make a choice according to loft, and the distance you are from the obstacle.

But how to achieve more height than your norm? Naturally, you proceed with more or less reverse strategies from the ones you use when hitting the ball low. Here are some of the adjustments to make from a normal shot when maximum quick height is the aim:
(1) Place the ball further forward in your stance, but only by an inch or so. This will increase the loft of your club at impact.
(2) Open the blade slightly. This gives more loft, and promotes fade, always a higher shot than a draw.
(3) Hold the club at the end of the grip.
(4) Incorporate a lively hand action into your swing.

**ABOVE:** Opening the blade increases the loft of the club, and is essential if you wish to play a cut-up shot.

**BELOW:** Shadows across the fairway can make it difficult to assess the distance of a shot.

A high-speed cut-up shot will get the ball up into the air very quickly and over the top of this obstacle.

(5)   Hit at full swing speed. This gives maximum backspin, and your ball will climb more quickly – provided you get a good strike.

(6)   Make sure your hands aren't ahead of the clubhead at impact. But a lively hand action will probably achieve this anyway.

When your obstacle is very close, but far less high – bushes, perhaps – and the green a short distance beyond, you can achieve amazing height, but minimal length, by adding two further ingredients.

Open the blade of your club much further, and swing across the target line, much as you would for a bunker or cut-up shot. With high swing speed you will get maximum backspin, and this added to sidespin, forces nearly all the ball's momentum to be directed upwards, rather than forwards.

However, because you are pushing your techniques to the ultimate, disasters are quite likely. You could get the heel of the club into the ball, rather than the middle, and end up with a shank. If the timing is different, you may meet the ball with the toe of your club.

This is a shot with a very high skill factor, and you really shouldn't try it unless you have practiced it a great deal.

# RULES AND COURSE BEHAVIOR

Thinking about course behavior, perhaps brisk play is the best courtesy you can offer the other players in your game, and also the other users of the course.

As you walk up to your ball, be making your mind up about club selection. Consult your yardage chart, if you carry one, as you walk along.

Professionals go about their business with reasonable speed for their tee shots, because the decision is a reasonably simple one. Length of shot is often not critical. The only things they have to consider is how to be sure to be short of a fairway bunker, or that a shot down the right hand side gives a better angle for a shot to the green. Changing weather conditions can make a difference, but practice rounds have probably taught them what to do beforehand.

Approaching the greens, however, many professionals set dreadful examples for club golfers. Not only do they not decide on club selection on their way to the ball, but they

**BELOW:** As you walk towards your ball, start thinking about your putt in order not to waste time on the green.

**BELOW:** Always leave the green immediately after you have finished playing the hole.

often appear not to give the matter any thought whatsoever as they wait for the other members of their grouping to play. Only then do consultation with caddies, tossing of grass into the air, and examination of charts begin.

Club golfers should ignore these sinners and try to emulate the briskness of a Tom Watson, an Ian Woosnam or a Lanny Wadkins. Even if you are a player who takes a long time to set up the ball and needs many waggles before you swing, there is no need to be slow-witted as well.

Order of play in a four-ball sometimes causes confusion, even though the convention is clear cut: furthest from the hole plays first. Minor troubles often arise from macho characters who do not like to admit that they are not nearest the hole, so haven't hit the longest drive.

But the longest drive is by no means necessarily the closest to the green, because the line of the tee shot is also significant. Quite a short tee shot, tight to the angle of a dogleg right, for example, may be much nearer than a longer drive going left. If you are a sensible golfer, however, you won't want to be making points about the length of your tee shot, and will merely wish to avoid playing out of turn. Just ask for agreement that it's your shot – or that it isn't.

Before you play, make sure that the game ahead is well out of range. This means not playing when your predecessors have left the green, but are still close to one side. You wouldn't hit a drive to a fairway with people a little off line but still within range: so it stands to reason that neither should you when playing to a green.

Most players are quiet enough when they are on the tee, close to a player about to tee off. However, remember, when you spread out on the course, that sound travels. Don't be too noisy with your clubs, and do not shout aloud in triumph or despair as you watch the result of your shot. There are other people on the course, perhaps about to tee off on another hole, or sink a downhiller with a testing borrow.

**ABOVE:** The longest drive is also the straightest so that player will play his approach shot first.

**ABOVE LEFT:** Always remove leaves and other loose impediments on your line as quickly as possible.

**BELOW:** Always replace your divots after playing from the fairway.

And when you've played – do replace your divot. Make sure that there's only one of them: that you haven't been scattering turf with your practice swings.

Like tee shots, shots from the fairway don't involve any particularly complicated rules, mainly because they are played from a well-prepared and well-defined part of the course. There are, however, rules which do become significant when you come upon unusual conditions.

## CASUAL WATER

This is water occurring anywhere other than in a water hazard. It is usually the result of winter conditions, or heavy rain in summer. You are in casual water if your ball lies there – or if you are standing in it. In that case, there need not be any surface water: if it wells up around the welts of your shoes you can declare 'casual water'.

In either case you can play the ball as it lies, or move to the nearest point, not nearer the hole, which avoids the conditions, and measuring one club length away, take a free drop. You are entitled to clean your ball before doing so.

**RIGHT:** If this casual water is on your line, you can move your ball to the nearest clear point on the green to give yourself an unimpeded putt.

**RIGHT:** You get a free drop when (casual) water rises above the welts of your shoes.

**ABOVE LEFT:** You get a free drop if your ball comes to rest on an area of the course marked GUR (Ground Under Repair).

**ABOVE RIGHT:** If your ball comes to rest on this new tee under construction you get a free drop.

## GROUND UNDER REPAIR

Exactly the same rules apply as for casual water. The only difference is that you are more likely to have a good lie under GUR, and many golfers forget that they are entitled to play the ball under these conditions.

## EMBEDDED BALL

You are entitled to relief when a ball is embedded in its own pitch mark, in any closely-mown area. But it must be its *own* pitch mark, and not an earlier one, and you must be sure that the hole in which you have come to rest *is* a pitch mark.

This can lead to arguments from time to time, usually from golfers wishing to claim relief when they're not entitled to it. However, there is a distinctive fresh appearance about a newly embedded ball situation.

## BURROWING ANIMALS

A golfer is entitled to relief from holes and scrapes made by burrowing animals. 'Does this mean,' you may well ask, 'any zoologically-produced hole or scrape?' No it does not.

Perhaps any contentious four-ball ought to be accompanied by a wildlife expert. Can you detect the difference between a scrape made by a rabbit, and one made by a dog? Neither can I, but it might be just as well to study the subject, because you can claim relief from animals which burrow into the ground to make their homes, but not from dogs, assumed by the R and A and the USGA to live above ground.

So if you know a variety of dog which burrows, and may spend the occasional night below ground (a Fox Terrier, perhaps) then you would be well placed to put a test case before golf's ruling bodies.

## UNUSUAL GROUND CONDITIONS

If a ball is embedded in its own pitchmark you get a free drop – but not if it is embedded in an old pitchmark.

The same rules apply here as for casual water and GUR. If you take a look at the fairway and surrounds of greens during a Tour event, you will find that the professionals have it a little easier than club golfers. They tend to demand a surface of approximately the same consistency as a very expensive carpet, apart from unavoidable divot holes, of course, and their wishes are often observed.

You will therefore note that many areas are ringed off by white lines. These are to show where the carpet has become a little threadbare, and indicate that the pro can drop off to more nearly perfect turf close by.

Much the same state of affairs exists at most golf clubs, except that the damage deemed to warrant such treatment is usually more severe. You certainly can't claim relief because you consider that you have a less-than-perfect lie after you've hit a magnificent 300-yard drive straight down the fairway – even if you think you deserve one.

## UNFIT BALL

If you've just thinned your tee shot, it's also likely that you have put a cut in your ball. Providing your fellow players

LEFT: An area of
ground circled with a
white line is deemed
GUR, so you would
be entitled to a free
drop if your ball
comes to rest in it.

agree, you can change it without penalty. If, however, they have reason to believe that you have already played with a damaged ball, perhaps because you were hitting over a water hazard, they are entitled to refuse consent. You will then have to wait until you have completed the hole.

## ADVICE VERSUS INFORMATION

You are entitled to ask any question you like about matters of fact (although not entitled to any answers). You may ask how many yards it is to the front or the green, or whether that is the flag you are playing to, for example, but you aren't allowed to ask those questions in an advice form.

You can say, 'How far is it to the green?' but not 'Will I reach the front of the green with my 5-iron?' or 'Is that the flag we're playing to?' but not 'With my high fade, will I stop it near the flag?'

There are all sorts of classic examples of this rule being broken throughout the long history of golf. In the 1896 British Open, James Kay signalled Harry Vardon to play short of a cross bunker in front of the last green at Muirfield. If Vardon had asked Kay, under the current rules of golf he would have been penalized for doing so (Kay had finished his round, and was a spectator). However, so the story goes, Kay was trying to force his opinions on Vardon by jumping up and down and waving his arms about. Since only about 20 people were watching (!) he must have been highly visible.

Vardon was never held responsible, because he hadn't asked for advice, and for all I know, didn't want any.

ABOVE: Again, the white line signifies GUR

More recently – now forgotten, but contentious at the time – in 1971, Arnold Palmer was playing with Gardner Dickinson against Peter Oosterhuis and Bernard Gallacher in the Ryder Club at Old Warson Country Club, St. Louis, Missouri. On a 208-yard hole, Palmer cracked an awesome 5-iron to the heart of the green.

Gallacher's caddie wasn't a pro, but simply a college boy there to earn a few dollars, and wasn't wise in the ways of golf. Mouth agape, he asked something like 'Holy Cow, Arnie! What club did you hit?' Palmer replied 'A 5-iron.'

That was enough for the British pairing to lose the hole for asking advice.

Arnold Palmer asked that the loss of hole penalty be forgotten – so perhaps *he* ought to have been disqualified. Why? Because he had himself broken the Rule of Golf which states that disqualification is the penalty for seeking to waive a Rule of Golf.

## OUT OF BOUNDS

Though most out-of-bounds shots are made from the tee, there are plenty of opportunities for the same thing to happen from the fairway. The procedure is much the same from the fairway, although you can't use a tee peg. You drop at the point the ball was hit, and add a penalty of stroke and distance to your score.

**BELOW:** The area to the left of the tee looks like it might be out of bounds. In fact it isn't. So, always consult the local rules when in doubt.

**LEFT:** If a sprinkler head interferes with your stance or stroke you are entitled to a free drop.

## LOST BALL

The procedure and penalty is the same as for a ball out of bounds. Remember, it is wise to play a provisional ball if there is a reasonable chance of your ball being lost.

## SPRINKLER HEADS

When these interfere with your stance or your stroke, you are entitled to drop away – but you're not obliged to.

## MOVING BALL

Always be aware that the action of grounding your club might cause your ball to move. Even on the fairway, avoid grounding

**ABOVE LEFT AND RIGHT:** A player lays his bag down having gone ahead to get a view of a distant flag. If he leaves the bag there on returning to his ball to play the shot, the bag now constitutes an illegal marker.

your club too firmly, very close to the ball. If in doubt, why ground it at all?

A moving ball is one which moves from its point of rest to another one, even if only by a small fraction of an inch. However, there's no penalty if your ball moves, but returns exactly to its original point of rest.

It's obviously far better to be careful in your actions around the ball, because any movement is open to dispute. The difference between a ball moving one-hundredth of an inch, and merely oscillating is a matter of opinion rather than fact, and so is a movement from the original point of rest and back to it.

## MARKING THE LINE

A golfer may, of course, use something that is already there to mark his line to the flag, but he musn't place something – a twig, for example – himself to help him line up and aim.

Such aids may occur accidentally. If a golfer labors to the top of a rise for a sight of the flag, chooses his club and then returns to his ball, he musn't leave his bag where it can act as a marker. Much the same applies if a caddie or partner indicates the line to the flag for a blind shot – and then remains there while the golfer hits.

There is an exception, of a kind, to this rule. The flag itself can be held aloft, above the hole, while you play.

The Rules of Golf are many and complicated, mainly as a result of the terrain over which the game is played. I do feel, however, that there would be no harm to the spirit of the game if this last one were to be abolished. If it's acceptable for an invisible flag to be made visible, then why shouldn't a marker be placed to show the direction of it?

But there it is.

# CARE OF THE IRONS

I irons are robust. Many players thump them into the ground, taking divots the size of soup plates with every shot. Most players take some turf, at least.

Very few of us protect the heads of our irons in the bag with woolly hats and the like, the way we do with woods. So they clink and rattle away merrily, getting scratched, and even chipped at times, every time we play a shot.

**BELOW:** After playing a fairway iron clear out any grass and mud from the grooves before playing your next shot with the club.

Irons need little care – but they do need some. Observe what happens at a tournament.

After every shot, the caddie cleans off every speck of grass and soil, either adhering to the clubface or forced into the grooves, as soon as the club is handed back to him. He knows that his player wants to hit the ball with the surface as it was made, and not with fragments of grass affecting the purity of impact.

You should do likewise, even though you probably won't have a body servant to do the job for you. You may not be a tournament professional, expecting to play with ultimate precision the next time you take the club from your bag, but why give yourself an unnecessary handicap?

The answer is to carry a simple 'maintenance kit'. This need be no more than a small piece of damp towelling, and ball cleaners are available – though these do tend to smear your golf ball rather than clean it afterwards. A sharp tee peg, or small pocket knife, may also be useful, especially in dry conditions when grass fragments become more difficult to remove.

Afterwards, your cleaning will already have been done. If not, a quick brush of the clubhead will do the job in moments. Shafts need very little attention indeed: a wipe over with a dry cloth if wet, or a damp cloth to remove mud, but it really matters very little if you ignore them altogether.

**RIGHT:** You are advised to protect your woods with headcovers whilst they are in the bag. Otherwise they will chink and rattle against each other during the course of a round, causing dents, nicks and scratches.

Scrubbing with a nylon brush will remove any grass and mud from the grooves on the faces of your clubs.

Grips are a different matter. They are the only contact you have with the club as a whole, and your hold on the club needs to be easily secure: it isn't helpful to have to hold on more firmly because the grips have become greasy, shiny or hard. Ideally, they should be cleaned after every round of golf, and certainly not left long without brief attention.

Cleaning is simple enough, with a small brush and just a little detergent. Rinse quickly and thoroughly. As wear continues over the months, this, eventually is not quite enough, and the effects of your treatment seem to last only for a short time. It is possible to prolong the life of your grips by rubbing them over with a very fine abrasive cloth, but the only real answer is to have them replaced.

It probably wasn't the grips that attracted you to the clubs in the first place. You bought the clubs for other reasons and simply accepted the grips as they were. Nowadays, however, you can make a choice from what your professional has on offer.

Tournament professionals are very fussy in this respect. Some like hard ones, some soft, and there are all sorts of materials with different textures to choose from. Don't forget to think how they are likely to perform in wet weather: some are very good, some become as slippery as eels.

So don't just go into the shop and say 'I want these re-gripped'. Take the time to decide which grips you prefer, and ask advice on such topics as wet weather performance and length of service. The cheapest, because of their short life, may turn out to be the most expensive.

Surface appearance of the club may not affect its performance. But loft certainly does.

The loft of some forged irons, and some others, can change with use. Also, dare I mention it, lofts are sometimes incorrect on brand new clubs.

You could, for example, have been wondering about your problems with, say, your 6- and 7-irons. When taking a shot to the green, you will often have spent time debating whether to use your 7-iron, but in the end, have chosen a 6-, just to be sure of being up.

Then, you may have found yourself short. In which case you will have wondered 'Should that really have been a 5-iron? The shot *felt* good. Perhaps my strike wasn't up to par.'

But perhaps you shouldn't have blamed your shot. Perhaps you should have blamed your club care.

Even when you buy a new set of clubs you should be aware of this factor. Get your professional to check the loft of every iron, just to be sure.

Obviously, you will be looking for evenly spaced lofts, giving you a range of distances all the way from 1- to 9-iron. (There could well be intentional differences as regards the sand iron and the wedge.)

However, even if the clubs were accurately set when new, lofts can change after a while. Perhaps the problem is caused by play on hard ground, or it could be that you have made contact with stones below the surface of the turf.

If the problem isn't too severe, your professional may be able to eliminate it for you, making sure that, in future, your 6-iron, for example, hits the ball some 15 yards further because it has a longer shaft and less loft.

But lofts aren't the only angle which should be checked. It's worth taking a look at the lies, too.

A lie, in this context, is governed by the angle between shaft and clubhead. It decides how the club sits on the ground.

Ideally, the sole of each club should rest evenly on the turf. The toe should not be more than a fraction off the ground, and even more important, it shouldn't sit lower than the heel of the club. If your clubs vary in this respect, you will be prone to draw shots with some clubs, and cut with others.

Unconsciously, you may adjust the way you set up to the ball, changing the way the club lies on the ground: lowering your hands a trifle will get the toe up, and raising them has the reverse effect. But this is no help at all if you want to play consistent golf. Your professional can easily make the appropriate checks, and adjustments can then be made.

Club golfers often don't bother, being defeatist enough to blame themselves, rather than their clubs. Sometimes, they're right, but touring professionals have a very different attitude. That's why, at tournaments, you may catch sight of a vast pantechnicon with a clubs manufacturer's name blazoned on it.

Obviously, there's an element of advertising about such a presence, but the manufacturer also goes along to cater to the needs of the touring professional who drops in for frequent changes of grip, and to have the lofts and lies of his clubs checked, and if necessary, altered.

He may also have changes made when the clubs are already 'correct'. 'Make that wedge stronger' he may say, and the technician will slightly reduce the loft. Or the instruction may be 'I'm not getting enough height on my 1-iron. Do something about it', in which case, the loft will be increased.

The professional may also find that he is drawing his iron shots when he wants to hit straight, or achieve a suspicion of fade. In this case, a change of lie is indicated.

Of course, we are talking here about golfers who are remarkable for their consistent full shot iron play, and perhaps you don't aspire to anything like the same precision. Nevertheless, it's unwise to persist with clubs which are a hindrance rather than a help to your golf.

It's a difficult enough game without that.

A recently cleaned iron – removing dirt will lessen the chance of a mis-hit and help to increase the degree of backspin imparted to the ball the next time you play a shot with the club.

# PRACTICE ROUTINES

The best time to increase the time you devote to practice is when you're playing well. Do so when you are in a bad spell, and the likelihood, even the certainty, is that all you will do is engrain a swing fault more and more deeply. Conversely, extra practice when you are playing well will build pluses into your muscle memory.

This is one reason why most tournament professionals spend so much time on the practice ground. As the pressure rises during competitive play, they want the muscle memory and confidence in their technique which enables them to play shots without conscious thought.

**LEFT:** Before practicing, always use a club to check the alignment of your stance with the target area.

On the practice ground, you, and they, may have one of two objectives. You may be trying to improve weak areas in your shot play, or you may be polishing the skills you already have. Of course, you could be trying to achieve both ends, but this depends on how much time you have to spare for practice. If your time is limited, it is probably sensible to concentrate on one objective or the other.

**One way to organize your practice is to go through the** bag from club to club. Start gently, working through the short irons, and on up to the driver, as you achieve satisfactory results with each.

Always choose a target, and especially when you are using the driver, don't make length your main aim. You are driving well when you can target your drives, and are hitting a consistent distance so that your practice shots are all coming to rest within quite a small area of the practice ground. Unless you have some compelling reason, don't spend more time with the driver than you do to pitching. Remember – if you are playing a steady game, the ability to play short irons close to the flag consistently will save far more shots than being able to drive a few extra yards.

Whichever club you are using, pause before each shot to think about what you are trying to achieve. Never hit ball after ball away mindlessly: that's not practice – it's merely exercise.

Always give great consideration to the shape of your shot and learn how to fade and draw the ball, and how to hit high and low.

Don't hit everything from the tee peg, or nudge your ball into a perfect lie. Encourage accurate striking by tramping your ball down a little, now and then – and don't forget to see how your ball travels from flying lies.

Out on the course, you will be playing some shots from deep and semi-rough. Many players only learn what they can achieve from these positions slowly from experience during play. Why not gain this experience on the practice ground?

How long should you practice? The main governing factor could be the length of time your interest endures, and that could change from day to day.

Little will be achieved if you're not keenly interested in the result of each shot you play on the practice ground. The less interested you are, the farther away you are from the real world of competitive golf on the course, whatever form it may take. Half an hour of peak effort and concentration is worth two hours of mindless, repetitive hitting.

You should also pay due attention to your physical fitness. To illustrate this, think of the world of track athletes, arguably the fittest section of the human race. Sometimes it seems that there isn't a well man or woman among them.

Consider the 10 years or so when British athletes dominated the 800- and 1500-metre distances. The names which spring readily to mind are Sebastion Coe, Steve Ovett, Steve Cram and Peter Elliot. Haven't they all, at one time or another, been stricken with viruses, stress fractures, strains? However fit you are, the human frame can only endure just so much stress.

It may appear that the most stressful activity a golfer has to endure is walking, as slowly as you like, up slopes of no great severity. But this isn't really so.

Professional golfers, especially those who practice intensely, overstress parts of their bodies. The lower spine. doesn't take kindly to the twisting it undergoes, even in the most elegant and rhythmic of golf swings. Hands, wrists, tendons, elbows, all complain as a result of pounding golf clubs into the turf for hour after hour.

When you feel a twinge – take note of the warning.

**TOP, CENTER AND LEFT:** Practicing shots from deep rough is a good hand-strengthening exercise – but it can be painful at times!

# WARMING UP

I suppose that a majority of golfers prepare for a round with a few swishes of the club on the first tee, and follow up by attempting to hit a drive for a quarter of a mile. Not many go to the practice ground to hit a few shots before they play in earnest. Yet, how useful that can be!

The routine can be quite short, and certainly shouldn't be long. Simply go quickly through the bag, from gentle pitch to drive. The aim isn't practice, but to get the feel of your swing, and accustom the fingers to the sensation of striking a ball.

Participants in most other sports and games warm up beforehand as a matter of routine, mainly to avoid cold muscles and unstretched sinews. Not that injuries from these causes are at all likely in golf.

If you warm up, you'll simply play better.

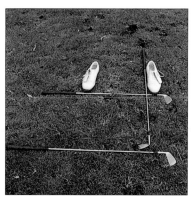

**TOP AND ABOVE:** Making use of clubs to check your alignment – although you don't have to get out of your shoes!

**BELOW:** When practicing, work your way, systematically, through every club in the bag.

**ABOVE:** A reward for diligent practice.

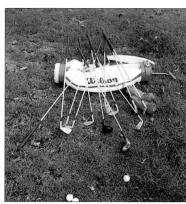

**ABOVE AND RIGHT:** A good leg position at the top of the backswing.

# ON THE
# GREEN

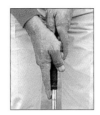

# GRIPS

I t's an old saying that more matches are won and lost on the green than anywhere else. A player who can get down in two putts rather than three will probably beat an opponent who can drive 50 yards farther. It follows, therefore, that anything you can do to eliminate that extra putt will pay huge dividends in terms of winning matches. And it all starts with the grip.

Palms opposed.

Adding the putter.

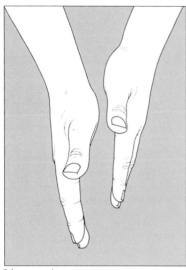
Palms opposed.

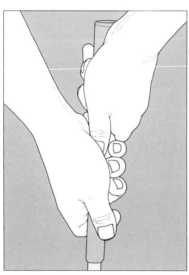
All fingers on the grip.

There is a tremendous variety of ways of holding the club when putting – you can get away with far more unorthodoxy than you ever can when playing full shots.

Nevertheless, you have to know the rules before you can break them with impunity, and there are certain basics which you ignore at your peril. For example, the vast majority of grips for putting are based on presenting the back of the left hand and the palm of the right hand to the hole; in other words, the palms are facing each other.

This gives you a very simple grip check. Simply place the palms together, with the club handle between them, and make sure that both are lined up squarely with the face of your putter.

You'll notice that this gives you one important variation on the way you grip the club for full shots: the top (left) hand will have moved counter-clockwise, while the right hand hasn't changed.

Having said that, many very good players don't change their grip at all, just because they have reached the green.

**Using the same grip on the greens as for long shots.**

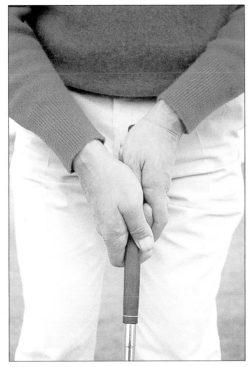

The reverse overlap in close up.

Reverse overlap grip – left forefinger

It can be argued that an unchanged grip feels more natural, and therefore more comfortable. I don't suppose that many golfers instinctively switch to different grips when putting. That probably comes when a player notices what other people are doing, and is spurred into starting to think about it all.

However, why change a winning system? If you find that a normal interlocking or overlapping grip works for you, then I certainly wouldn't be the one to tell you to alter it.

Even so, let's assume that the 'palms-opposed' grip works best for most people and proceed from there. It's sensible to start with the standard grip, and go into a few variations later on.

Because many golfers like to feel that the right hand provides the strike while the left is there principally to support the club, they tend to make sure that all fingers are gripping the club. This, of course, means that the right hand slips down the club a little, and the right little finger no longer overlaps the left forefinger.

Instead, the left hand does some overlapping of its own. It has also slipped a little way down the club, and the left forefinger has come to rest over the bottom hand.

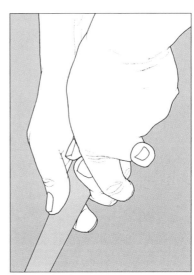

Reverse overlap grip.

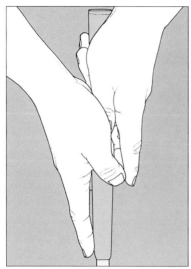

Both forefingers extended.

Extending both forefingers.

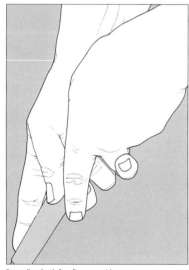

Extending both forefingers – side on.

Just where it comes to rest is largely a matter of personal preference. It can find itself over the little finger of the bottom hand, or at the other extreme, travel downwards until it overlaps the fingertips of the bottom hand. Most people will find that a happy medium works best: somewhere over the knuckles of the right hand.

This is called the 'reverse overlap grip' because it reverses the overlap used for full shots. As always, the object is to encourage the hands to work as one unit.

Extending that forefinger downwards is also helpful in another way. Very slightly, it tightens the sinews of the left wrist, giving a firmer feel to the putting stroke. You'll appreciate just how important this is a little later on.

## REVERSE OVERLAP – VARIATIONS

There are a round half-dozen variations of the standard reverse overlap grip. Let's take a look at them.

(1) Don't extend the left forefinger. Just let it come to rest on the putter grip. But don't forget – you do lose that slight tightening of the left wrist.

**ABOVE LEFT:** Split hands putting.

**ABOVE RIGHT:** An extreme of the split-hands method.

(2)   The right finger, quite naturally, falls into much the same position for putting as for any other shot. Some good players, however, like to curl it around the handle, while others position it far more loosely, with only the inside of the knuckle in contact. Most people will find the second of these alternatives more successful, because it helps to relax the arm muscles. There is, however, another alternative . . .

(3)   Extend the right forefinger more or less vertically down the handle. This means that both forefingers are now pointing downwards, helping to take the wrists out of the putting stroke, and providing a much more 'arms-only' movement.

This is perhaps the greatest single difference between the basic method used by modern players, when compared with great putters of the past. Walter Hagen and Bobby Jones, for example, were far more wristy than their present-day counterparts.

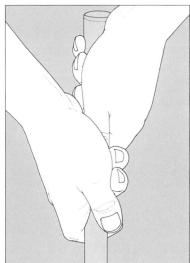

Vardon grip.

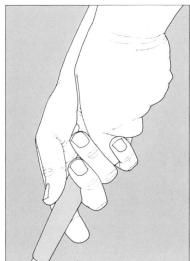

Vardon grip – side on.

**LEFT:** A green close to water will tend to be damper and putt more slowly.

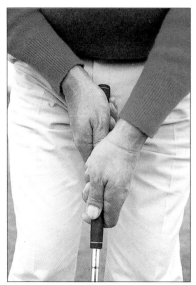

Putting with reversed hands.

It worked superbly for them, but lesser mortals are far better off when this particular source of movement is eliminated from their putting action. Ben Crenshaw provides the clearest example of the arms-only modern method.

Some players like to make that right forefinger the focus of their putting stroke. They like to 'feel' it tapping the ball, and continuing along the target line into the hole.

(4)  Just *where* you place your grip on the club handle is very important indeed, because it affects the feel of the club enormously. At one extreme, that great putter Ray Floyd holds the club at the top of the handle and stands tall as well. Not only that, but he also uses a longer-than-standard shaft.

Other great players like to get nearer to the ball. For example, at the turn of the century, the two greatest names in the game were Harry Vardon and J H Taylor. It has to be said that Vardon wasn't really a better-than-average putter, but, obviously, each of them had legions of imitators. Because both crouched low over the ball when putting, everyone was doing it in no time at all – and the fashion didn't really change until the 1920s.

Bobby Jones, undoubtedly the greatest golfer in the world, came along and putted magnificently, standing comfortably upright. The world duly took note.

Still – if you feel like crouching, you have an excellent alibi for so doing. Andy North does, hands absurdly far down the club, and he's won the US Open twice!)

(5)  Almost as extreme is the practice of leaving the left hand where it is, and setting the bottom hand low down on

Putters come in different shapes. When buying one, make sure you feel comfortable with it; the type of putter head does not matter.

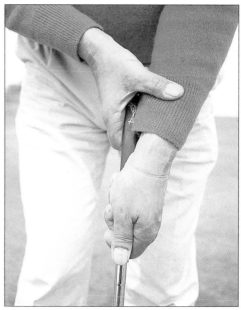

The left wrist has broken.

The Langer grip, not generally recommended, but this really ensures the left wrist doesn't break.

the handle, leaving a gap between the hands. This invariably means that the ball strike comes exclusively from the right hand, and that the left is simply there to steady the club. Personally, I don't think this method will help the vast majority of golfers.

Even so, there is a notable devotee of the method in Hubert Green.

Ray Floyd may well use a longer-than-standard putter, but some go a great deal further in using a gigantic club with one grip at the top of the shaft and another halfway down, leaving a gap of about a couple of feet between the hands.

If you are a thoroughly bad putter, it could be worth trying one of these monsters, which are a common sight on the US Senior Tour.

Golfers who have passed their 50th birthday often find such a club a partial cure for the putting yips, but don't think that this agonising problem is the exclusive prerogative of the older player. Sandy Lyle used one for a while early in the 1990 American season, while Sam Torrance, who many had dismissed as on his way out on the European Tour, found that the club was a good enough yip cure to enable him to make the 1989 Ryder Cup team.

(6) To go to the ultimate extreme, there is no law of golf which says you have to have both hands on the club at all, and nothing to say which of the two hands you may use.

I can remember one tournament golfer who used his right hand alone, and employed a very short putter. But – a word of warning – while his method was certainly interesting, it never enabled him to make putting a strong feature of his game. Admittedly, there have been tournament winners who putted with the right hand only. But not for long: it only takes a few mis-hits to destroy confidence in the method, probably forever.

## REVERSED HANDS

Some 30 years ago, a South African golfer named Sewsunker Sewgolum caused amazement by winning European tournaments. The raised eyebrows were prompted by the fact that, although right-handed, and standing to the ball that way, he placed his left hand below the right for all shots.

Many children grip the club that way quite naturally, and parents and club professionals are very quick to tell them that you just can't play golf that way. Apart from anything else, the grip isn't much help to most people when it comes to a full swing.

Obviously, no one had told Sewgolum that, and he did go around winning tournaments.

Nevertheless, although this reverse grip isn't suitable for most aspects of play, it can be used successfully on the green. Peter Alliss, Tom Kite, Tony Jacklin and Bernhard Langer, for example, have used the reversed hands method profitably for long periods.

In most cases, the grip is used when the player concerned has developed a nervous tremor in the putting stroke. The method brings into play a whole new set of small muscles, and seems to help eliminate, or at least, ameliorate, the problem.

So it's something to try if you're suffering from mental turmoil on the greens. There are, however, other advantages. In brief, it's worth the experiment if nothing else seems to work.

This is mainly because the commonest fault in putting is the breaking of the left wrist, just before the ball is struck, leading to very inconsistent putting. The left-below-right grip minimizes the likelihood of this happening, because it feels natural to pull the club through with the left hand and arm.

If you think 'pull' to yourself, you won't flick the left hand and wrist at the ball, and if the left wrist is firm, then that's one variable you have eliminated from your game.

Greenside bunkers make approach shots difficult, but the flagstick is well positioned on this green and, once on the putting surface, a standard 'two putt' should be no problem.

# CHOOSING A PUTTER

**B**efore sitting down to write this chapter, I conducted a very small piece of research. I visited my pro's shop and counted just how many different types of putter they could offer me. The total was a staggering 113 clubs in 47 different models, the differences between them ranging from the fundamental to the insignificant.

So what does Mr or Ms Beginner do when faced with such a bewildering array of choices? Probably pick out one or two and waft them about in the air, I should think, and then probably try them out on a strip of carpet to see which works best.

Because of the large choice of putters available, your local professional will be only too pleased to let you try them out before making your purchase.

A putter, plus a wood and either the four even or five odd numbers make up a half-set of irons.

Which is all very well, but not nearly enough like the real world to serve any useful purpose.

To start with, no strip of carpet is anything like a green, be it ever so well manicured. Furthermore, the distance between the edge of the green and the hole is very much longer than the pro's floor covering. To see how a putter performs, you really must try it away from the cosy haven of the shop, on the green itself.

This is where supporting your club pro, rather than a sports shop or a department store, really pays off. After all, the average shopkeeper won't be very keen on watching you disappear over the horizon with an armful of sample putters. In contrast, your pro will almost certainly encourage you to try out a club or two on the practice green, possibly taping the clubhead to prevent scratches.

Alternatively, you could avoid worrying him by experimenting with the selection of used clubs which will invariably be in stock. In addition, you could take any opportunity to try putters belonging to your fellow golfers.

All this is infinitely preferable to yielding to impulse and buying putter after putter in the hope that the law of averages will, sooner or later, produce your own, individual, magic wand.

The only way to get a feel for certain features of these clubs is to experiment at every possible opportunity. For example, if you eventually come to prefer standing fairly

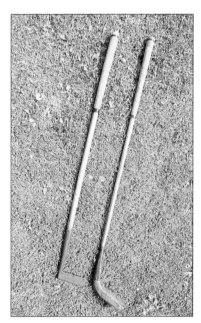

Two of the earliest known types of putter. The one on the left is very heavy and the wooden one is far longer in the shaft than would find favor with today's golfers.

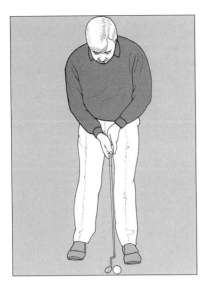
Reverse overlap grip.

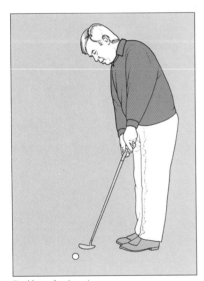
Double overlapping grip.

This putter is similar to those used at the turn of the century by such great players as Harry Vardon, James Braid and John B. Taylor.

upright to the ball, you'll probably need a putter with a shaft of above-average length, and if it's not upright in lie, you'll find yourself stubbing the toe. Conversely, the reverse applies if you crouch over the ball, or prefer standing with your hands close to your body.

Weight is another vital consideration. Some players come to prefer a heavy head, enabling you always to strike the ball gently, unless you're faced with a long putt. Others hold the reverse opinion, finding that heavy clubs seem likely to send the ball streaking past the hole, and that they can never bring themselves to swing the club at all freely.

Which are you? Only experiment will tell. Just as important, you will want to avoid buying a club which doesn't really suit your style, and which leads to adjusting your method to suit the club you've chosen.

All these things seem very obvious when they're written down, but many, many golfers go through their entire golfing lives without such basic principles even occurring to them. The words to remember are 'lie, length and weight'. They apply whichever make or model of club you try, ranging from the most traditional to the strangest of new patents.

What about the flex of the shaft? There isn't really any need to get too complicated about this: extreme flex combined with a heavy head is to be avoided, and so is a rigid shaft and a light head, which can make you feel you're playing with a stick in your hands. I suspect, however, that the average golfer is unaware of the characteristics of his or her putter shaft, and perhaps that's as it should be. What you don't know about, won't worry you.

An undulating two-tier green well protected by a ditch.

## PUTTER TYPES

In common with all other conventional golf clubs, the first putters were made of wood, although iron putters soon arrived on the scene. Wood reigned supreme throughout the 19th century, however, and putters looked very much like the drivers and fairway woods of the time. Greens were rough, by modern standards, and putters had whippy shafts and needed quite a long sweeping swing to be effective. About three inches shorter than today, putters were very much flatter in lie, so the player needed to stand well away from the ball. Before pitching clubs were introduced, putters were often used from many yards short of the green.

A modern day metal-headed putter. The head is heavier than most putters but many golfers prefer a putter with weight in the clubhead.

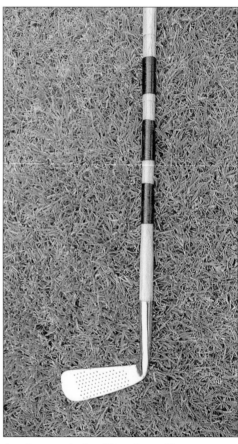

A modern reproduction of the putter used by Bobby Jones.

As the century wound on, and irons became increasingly popular, it was natural that metal should be used for putters as well. The wooden club gradually faded out, but when white metal heads became all the rage, some models retained the traditional shape of the head of the wooden model. This kind of head still survives, notably in the shape of the Ray Cook and other models. In putting, as in most other items of golf equipment, there is seldom anything entirely new under the sun.

Iron clubs eventually took over, and except for the length of the shaft and loft, they didn't look so very different from a 1-iron. Both, until the 1930s, had hickory shafts and putters were usually much lighter, and considerably more lofted, than those in use today. This type still survives, usually with a flange along the back to provide more weight.

It may surprise you to learn that the center shaft was first used early this century; the American, Walter Travis used one when winning the British Amateur Championship in 1904. It was called the 'Schenectady', and was regarded as a magic club. Perhaps the Royal and Ancient thought it unfair for they banned it a few years later. The ban lasted about 40 years, although center shafts continued to be used in countries which adhered to the rules of golf as decreed by the United States Golf Association.

Today, most putters have the shaft attached at some point between the heel and the center of the club, rather than at the heel itself, the basic idea being that putting is easier if you are striking the ball fairly close to the end of the shaft. This is certainly something well worth thinking about.

In the 1960s the American, Karsten Solheim, invented what is arguably the most revolutionary putter of all. He realized that many putts which finish short of the hole aren't a matter of misjudgement of length, so much as failure to strike the ball with the right part of the club, and on many traditional putters, that 'sweet spot' is very small indeed.

He solved this problem by placing most of the weight towards the heel and toe, providing a worthwhile margin for error in the middle where one hadn't existed before.

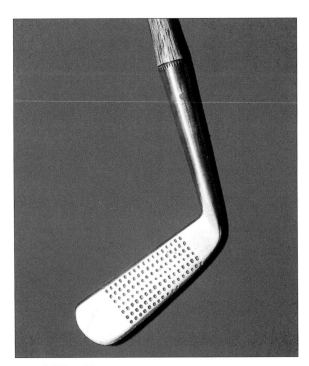

**ABOVE:** A 1920s putter.

Most golf clubs have practice greens which are manicured the same as the putting surface on the course. You are advised to spend ten minutes or so on the practice green before starting your round. That way you will get the 'feel' of the greens.

Of course, in Solheim's 'Ping' clubs, there is still an optimum spot with which to strike the ball, but if you fail to find it, a slight mis-hit gets you closer to the hole than you would have been with a blade putter.

When you watch tournament players, take note of the surprising number of them who use either 'Ping' putters, or some other heel-and-toe weighted designs.

If you want to make a living from the game, then good putting is an essential, and you'll be aware that many events are won by the player whose game is in good order, and who also turns out to be the best putter of the week.

There are very few professionals who haven't tried out hundreds of putters, so they have much more information on the subject than most of us. What they eventually use is therefore much more significant than the more casual choices of club golfers.

'Trying out' is one thing, but building up a stock of them is expensive, and I don't advise it. Think of Bernhard Langer, for example, renowned for his gallant, though temporary, conquests of his extreme problems on the green. He didn't really become a force to be reckoned with until he found a

BELOW: Lead tape has also been added to this putter, but the cutaway behind the face makes an ideal place for adding 'extra weight'.

ABOVE: To gain extra weight to the clubhead the reverse of the face has leaded tape added to it.

**LEFT:** The Goose Neck (or Wry-Neck) putter is one of the most popular types of putter. The line of the shaft, when looking down it from the putting position, is slightly in advance of the putter head. This picture shows the rear of the clubhead. Note the white mark, which acts as an aid to lining up the club with the ball.

**RIGHT:** A Center-Shafted putter. Again, notice the nick on the top of the club face; the ball should be lined up with that mark when putting.

putter which suited him. But things only seemed to work for a while; whatever he tried, his nervous twitch invariably came back to haunt him. Nowadays he admits to owning 70 putters.

And if, like most of us, you consider that to be a large number, spare a thought for Arnold Palmer. He has 3,000 of them!

The great Palmer years were – let's say – 1958-64, a period when he was famous for his bold and highly effective putting. After that, his skills began to wane, and his putter collection grew, as he tried to retrieve the situation by buying putters galore, or trying clubs sent to him by admirers. Surprisingly, Palmer would have very little to do with new and innovative designs: most of his 3,000 are of the blade type with a rear flange. Palmer still likes to spend time in his workshop modifying some of his putters. He'll alter lofts, lies, weights and, by judicious use of a file, even shapes.

I don't suggest that this sort of activity will turn you into another Arnold Palmer, but such modification is worth considering. You may have noticed that your feel for weight can vary from day to day. If, for example, a putter begins to feel too light for you, then there's an easy remedy. Simply add some lead tape.

The type of putter favored by many of the modern-day professionals. Note the yellow and red 'T' marker. This helps to line the ball up correctly at address.

A basic Blade Putter with no marker on the top of the club face. This may be worth considering when buying a putter.

It's surprising how few club players make use of this invaluable commodity, but take a look in a professional's bag and you'll find a very different story. Some pro's actually stick lead tape to *every* club, believing that they can 'fine tune' each to their own requirements by so doing. That may be going a bit far for most of us.

I wouldn't advise filing a putter, if only because the resale value might be reduced to nil. Club pro's will help you by altering the lie of a club, however, ensuring that it sits on the ground in mid-sole. Remember, also that you shouldn't have to move near to or further away from the ball because heel or toe is catching the turf.

Loft can also be altered, although the type of metal used may prevent this; manganese bronze, for example, has to be worked at very high temperatures.

All very interesting, but if you can find a club which suits you without alteration, then stick to it.

This Blade Putter clearly shows that modern-day putters do not have 'dimples' or grooves, unlike the hickory-shafted putter of yesteryear.

Putters past and present. While all different, the one thing they have in common is the face of club being at right angles to the floor.

A blade putter with hickory shaft and a very large-headed putter which became popular after Jack Nicklaus used one whilst winning the 1986 US Masters.

A Basakwerd putter. One of the oddest designs – yes, the toe does point towards your own toes when you use one.

# CHOOSING A BALL

Golfers tend to be obsessed by length. Most will buy a ball which they think will carry and run the furthest. In contrast, the average tournament pro can hit it quite far enough for all practical purposes, enabling them to use an iron from the tee, and still reach the green on shorter par 5's with another iron club. They don't, therefore, choose for length, but rather for the amount of control a ball will give them. (Having said that, it's worth remembering that a good many of them are under contract to play a particular brand of ball, and receive bonuses for winning with it.)

Control arises from the ability to impart spin, A balata-covered ball will take much more spin than a solid one, providing more backspin and making it easier to draw or fade the ball. Some prefer a solid ball, however, relishing the definite feel it gives to the clubface. I remember Henry Cotton once remarking to me that he would have loved to have had the modern hard ball to putt with.

Cotton felt it would have helped him with problems on the greens, so the choice is worth thinking about. Do you prefer the feel of a harder or softer ball when putting? It could make all the difference.

Golf ball cleaners are inexpensive to buy and it is worth carrying one in your golf bag. Make sure your ball is clean before you putt. You can only lift the ball off the putting surface to clean it.

Golf balls come in varying colors. The traditional white ball remains the most popular and is the one that is used in competitive golf. When there is snow around a colored ball is recommended.

# CARE OF THE PUTTER

Most putters are made of reasonably hard metal, some very hard indeed. Such heads need very little protection, so not a few golfers use head covers to keep the club in a new condition.

Very little maintenance is needed because the putting stroke itself is hardly likely to do the club any injury.

Occasional attention to the grip is advisable. The putter is used more than any other club, so there is friction to smooth the surface and a gradual accumulation of grease and dirt.

Besides the condition of the putter grip, you might also consider a change. A great variety of shapes are available and it could be – at the simplest level – that a change from round to square, or vice versa, might be helpful.

Even if you can't see it, greens usually slope towards lower ground.

# GETTING DOWN TO IT

N ow – you've chosen your putter, and you have sorted out your grip. All you have to do now, is get out on the green and start getting the ball into the hole. Let's start with . . .

An exposed green will often putt faster than others because the wind dries it out quickly.

# GRIP PRESSURE

Seve Ballesteros maintains that you should only hold a club firmly enough to stop it falling out of your hands. And that's for a *full* shot, where the clubhead may be moving at well over 100 miles per hour.

It follows, therefore, even allowing for Seve's genius, that there is absolutely no excuse for clinging on grimly, knuckles whitened, when you're indulging in the gentle art of putting. After all, you really only apply much force when you're using your putter as a 'Texas wedge', choosing to putt from well short of the green.

For some players, there can be an exception to the rule. When taking a short putt – say four feet or less – firming up the grip can help a more decisive stroke, and prevent the blade from wavering, becoming just a little more open or closed.

Trying to find the sweet spot.

An open, wide stance of around 1900.

For most of us, most of the time, however, touch is the name of the game. When muscles of fore and upper arm tighten – feel vanishes.

## EXACT STRIKING

You know that glorious feeling. The one when the ball flies off an iron or wood, as sweetly as a bird. No jarring in the fingertips at all, and a stark contrast to the sensation one gets when hitting a full 1-iron on the bottom of the blade on an icy morning!

Obviously, you've found the sweet spot on the clubface. Everyone searches for that sensation on full shots, but how many of us even consider the matter when putting?

But – knowing where that 'sweet spot' is on your putter, and bringing it into contact with the ball, can save you shot after shot on the green.

Let's suppose you are facing a ten-yard putt, and have judged the pace and borrows of the green to perfection, and that your clubhead moves at exactly the pace you've decided upon. Then your ball will drop neatly into the hole. Obviously. I'm afraid not. Unless the strike from the sweet spot is perfect, you'll finish feet short.

So first you have to find out where that sweet spot actually *is*. Fortunately, that's not too difficult. Take a ball, preferably a hard one, and bounce it a good few times on your putter face. Because you're doing this randomly, you'll notice a fair amount of vibration along your putter handle. When you don't – you've found the sweet spot.

Having done that, you can then bounce the ball more carefully, until you've located the spot precisely. You can then mark it temporarily, remembering to make your mark more permanent, perhaps by making a nick at the top of the blade, a little later.

The obvious assumption is that you should be hitting any shot from what looks like the middle of the clubface, but this is often not so, and you'll probably need a little practice to adjust to the new position.

The putter on the left is standard length. That on the right encourages an upright stance for a tall golfer.

## THE STANCE

Many great putters have adopted a very open stance, while others have stood in a closed position. They will all have

**ABOVE:** A jab putt, no follow-through.

**RIGHT:** This green is far from perfect. Assess the green's 'feel' when you first walk on to it and decide whether it is going to make your putt faster or slower. Don't forget, you are not allowed practice putts on the green.

made their choice after a great deal of experimentation. For most of us, however, a square stance will work best. This means that both toe tips will be parallel to the target line, between the ball and the point you're aiming at – which isn't necessarily the hole, when allowing for borrow.

Your distance from the ball will depend on a variety of factors, including length of putter shaft, your height, and whether you hold your hands high or low.

The ball itself may lie anywhere between the middle of the feet to a little ahead of the left foot – two extremes which have been used by a few successful players. Most players find a position somewhere opposite the left heel works best.

## ANGLE OF ATTACK

The direction the putter head is travelling in when it strikes the ball is obviously important, but the angle of its path is equally so. There are only three possibilities – level, descending and rising. Great putters have used all three very successfully, but there are advantages and disadvantages with all three.

Take Gary Player. In spite of the fact that most players think they ought to get down in two from a reasonable position in a green-side bunker, the great South African will probably go down in history as the finest bunker player ever. He was, and is, superb from the sand, but the sheer quality of his short putting makes him look even better. After all, you can't get down in two if you miss the putt!

Player is one of the very few great putters whose clubhead is descending when it meets the ball. His short follow through makes the shot look like a jab.

**ABOVE AND RIGHT:** Sometimes you have to putt from an unusual stance. Grip down the shaft if you get in this position.

For most putters, the major advantage of the descending angle of attack is that a momentary backspin is imparted which takes some speed off the ball and enables it to be struck more definitely. This, however, becomes a disadvantage as putts get longer. Once feel for distance becomes involved, that jabbing action can't work for many people.

In 1987, Nick Faldo came in from the cold and won the Open at Muirfield. Over the next few years, as he added two US Masters titles, came within a whisker of the 1990 US Open, and won the 1990 British Open, we heard a great deal about his new swing developed with coach, David Leadbetter.

Faldo had always had a good long game, but inside himself, hadn't really believed that it was consistent enough when under extreme pressure. Faldo's 'new' swing is now part of legend, but his putting is equally remarkable.

There isn't much drama in watching a man hole out from four feet. It's exactly what everyone, from tournament professional to modest club player, is expected to do. The point is, that most *don't*.

Except Nick Faldo. He must, obviously, miss sometimes, especially from those fast downhillers with a drift to one side, but those apart. Faldo is, and has long been, arguably the best short putter the world has seen.

From whatever distance, Faldo's ideas about striking are the same, and diametrically opposed to those of Gary Player. His putting swing paths involve a low away swing, and meeting the ball at the equator, with the clubhead travelling upwards. He believes that this imparts topspin, and helps to get the ball rolling, rather than hopping, along quickly. This means a more gentle approach than the Player method, and gives Faldo the feel of stroking all his putts.

Nick Faldo often practices putting with a wedge, making sure that the upwards angle is maintained. If he swings through too low, he will produce a chip shot, making the ball leave the ground for a foot or two. If he makes contact in the middle, with the leading edge of the club travelling upwards, the ball will hug the ground, just as it does when using a putter.

Both of these methods work, for Player and Faldo and many others. Equally, great numbers of golfers have believed that there is no substitute for making the club follow low through the ball and on along the target line.

This is certainly an easier route to consistency. The other

When putting to the upper tier of a green, concentrate on distance rather than accuracy. If you don't strike the ball firmly enough, it may well end up back at your feet!

The Nicklaus position of the right elbow.

Putter grounded.

Putting with the sole off the ground.

two methods involve trying to deliver a glancing blow, imparting backspin or topspin, while keeping the clubhead low to the ground before and after impact with the ball does not. The only answer is to experiment to see which method suits you best.

## HOW LOW?

Most of this is entirely obvious. The clubhead mustn't brush the grass because the merest suggestion of a bump, and the club, brushing against the grain of the green, will be checked more severely than you might think.

However, many players start from a position with the club resting on the ground. You can't really swing back from that position, because the first movement has to be to lift the club from the ground before swinging back, or to move back with a swing which is partly lift.

# HEAD AND EYE

It's ideal to have the feeling that you are looking from behind the ball, along the target line. This is very much the position which Jack Nicklaus adopts, and his confidence in his method has enabled him to last for well over 30 years in competitive golf. In his great years, he very seldom had miracle days on the greens, but he always seemed to have the knack of holing the ones which really mattered.

Many golfers, however, won't find themselves happy with the Nicklaus position. It seems more natural to have the head over the ball, but – remember – don't just look at the top of it. That will slightly, but perhaps fatally, affect your feel for the stroke. After all, you are going to have to hit the *back* of the ball, not the *top* of it.

When preparing to make your putt, you will, inevitably, be taking one or two glances along the line. Taking too many is valueless, however; it just delays the 'moment of truth' when you have to hit the ball.

Looking along the line.

# EVERY PUTT IS STRAIGHT

All TV watchers will have sometimes been amazed at the vast swing of the ball seen on the fast greens of the US Masters and Open. Even the much slower British greens can sometimes give a freakishly big swing, as when putting over some of the humps at St Andrews. Even so, the player should always think of these as straight putts: the ball is hit straight, the green provides the ball's lateral movement.

Low follow-through.

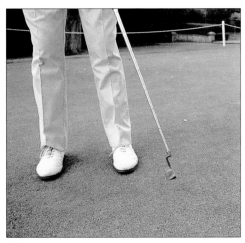

Club more on the rise here.

Plum bobbing standing behind the line.

Plum bobbing crouching behind the line.

LEFT: The two levels on this green add
to difficulties of putting.

**LEFT TO RIGHT, TOP TO BOTTOM:** Medium-length putt with slight borrow from the left. This one fell short.

Nevertheless, your thinking has to change on any green with borrow. Let's take the short ones first – from, say, two feet to five feet.

The best method is to visualize the curve your ball will need to take, and the ideal pace for it to travel. The ball is then started on its way straight, aimed at a point along that curving path.

You can, however, take a very different attitude to the curving short putt, simply straightening the curve.

A ball borrows more when it is travelling very slowly. We've all seen that trickling ball move sharply sideways across the front of the hole, just when it seemed to be about to topple in at its last gasp. A brave putter simplifies things by hitting the ball more crisply.

Rather than aim at, perhaps, four inches from the hole when putting delicately, they know there will be little turn on a firm putt from close range. They might be able to aim just inside a lip.

Of course, there are perils. It's fatally easy, on a downhill putt on a fast green, for you to finish up further from the hole than you when you started – if you miss. So don't.

Unless confidence is high, however, most players discard this approach for a fast downhill putt. It's probably better to dribble the ball at the hole, in the knowledge that,

The high spots on greens dry out in hot weather (brown areas). Your ball will run more freely over these parts.

if you miss, you'll only be two or three feet beyond the hole, at worst.

For a medium-length putt (10–15 feet) your strategy needn't change much. However, even when putting firmly, you'll see that any borrow will start to take effect. You'll certainly be aiming outside the hole, but being firm still has the same advantages; a dying ball is a dying ball, and it will borrow just as much, however far it has travelled. A firm putt still makes the putt straighter.

Long putts present different problems of course. The thought processes are different when we say that every putt is straight. In this case you need to visualize the curving line of your ball, but it will still travel in a relatively straight line when it is travelling quickly. Try to hit straight along your chosen line, aiming at something – perhaps a lighter or darker blade of grass – and feel the pace that your ball should be travelling when it arrives there.

# MOVING PARTS

I t has long been a truism of design that a well-engineered
mechanism should have as few moving parts as possible.
The same applies to the golf swing and, it follows, to the
mini-swing that is the putting stroke.

As far as putting is concerned, the great golfers of the
distant past were very wristy. They often saw putting as a
matter of hinging the wrists to and fro, only allowing the arms
to come into it for very long putts. Such ideas have long been
discarded, and even reversed. Nowadays, the wrists only
break when the distance to the hole is very great.

For at least a generation, from the end of World War I
until the 1930s, Bobby Jones and Walter Hagen were the

Although this isn't a true two-tier green, this player would have found putting from further down the upslope difficult to judge.

models, simply because their stature as the two greatest golfers in the world was unassailable. They remained just as influential after they had disappeared from the scene, because no one in their class appeared for about ten years. Even when Henry Cotton, in Britain, and Sam Snead, Byron Nelson and Ben Hogan, in the United States, arrived, in the years either side of World War II, nothing much changed.

This was because Jones and Hagen were supreme putters and their successors didn't seem to be. Cotton never looked comfortable on the greens. Although he was competent, his success was invariably attributed to the rest of his game.

In the United States things were much the same. From 1944, Nelson produced an unerring straightness which no one has been able to match since, and which was probably paralleled only by Harry Vardon in his great years from 1896 to 1900. He didn't miss short ones, and didn't three-putt very often, but people saw him as a great golfer, not a great putter.

When Ben Hogan reached his peak from 1946 to 1953 or so, it was his long game people noticed. A few observers thought he was deadly from about eight feet or so, but that was it. He was very like Henry Cotton, in that both made full shots look easy, but neither was much imitated for their putting abilities.

Much the same can be said for Samuel Jackson Snead. He had the most oily and powerful swing ever seen, and his short game was every bit as good – apart from his short putting. Snead was superb on the greens from long range, but, so they say, was always likely to twitch from close to the hole. You couldn't emulate his long game, and his putting failings were to be avoided.

It took Bob Charles to change ideas about putting. Bob wasn't a bad golfer at all, even though he was left-handed, which always looks awkward and 'different'. His game was long enough – as opposed to 'long' – off the tee, and people, including his fellow professionals, considered him to be just an average golfer. So why was he so successful?

The answer, surely, lay in his putting. People who failed to take note of his consistency on the fairway sat up and took notice when the New Zealander reached the green.

Bob Charles really did have a new putting secret. He took the wrists out of the putting stroke. He imagined that his mini-swing came from his neck; from a joint just above the shoulders, and he *didn't break his wrists*.

Today, all the pro's believe the same, although they may have different ways of expressing the concept. Even when

Don't putt into bunkers! It's often been done here – the Road bunker at St Andrews.

**The Ben Crenshaw arm position.**

Keep that flow of the left elbow constant.

tapping it in from two inches, they use an arms-only movement and *don't break the wrists*.

Oddly enough, the most effective golfer of all time has been much less imitated. For many years, Jack Nicklaus was regarded as no more than an overweight, crew-cut kid who could lash the ball huge distances, and then muddle through everywhere else. In fact, Jack, himself, now sees his golf game that way through the '60s and into the following decade.

While he may not have been the longest hitter in the world, there weren't many who were longer, and most of *them* couldn't play the game at all the rest of the way. But it was years before many people realized just how good Nicklaus was on the greens.

Jack's great strengths were the ability to hit a vast distance, and then follow up with superb long irons, and mid-irons that were just about as good. After that, he showed no more than average pro talent – until it came to putting.

The Nicklaus method is still like no one else's. Mechanically, he seems to stand behind the ball, thrusting towards the hole with a right-hand-dominated stroke. Even so, it isn't a matter of hand action; rather a piston movement, from the shoulders with the left arm unbending, and the right side providing the momentum.

Ben Crenshaw emerged early in the 1970s and, although his game was different, was hailed as the new Nicklaus. It hasn't quite worked out for him, largely because of a tendency to hit wild long shots. As a consequence, he has earned a reputation as the best player of recovery shots on the US Tour. Fellow professionals think equally highly of his putting.

Unlike Jack Nicklaus, Crenshaw has seen his putting stroke widely imitated. He stands further away from the ball than most, and is different from Bob Charles in that his stroke looks arms-only. His method has enabled him to be a winner into the 1990s and has brought him one US Masters.

Like many professional, Ben Crenshaw has a collection of putters. Being a student of the history of the game, however, most of them are antiques. While playing, he has remained faithful to an early love; a Wilson 8802, which is a blade putter with a rear flange. As I've said before, if you find a putter you are happy with – stick to it.

But Ben could probably putt well with just about anything. During his Ryder Cup singles battle with Eamonn Darcy at Muirfield in 1987, he broke his putter shaft after just a few holes. A complete disaster, you may think, but although he eventually lost, it was his long game which let him down. He seemed to putt just as well with an iron.

Among top-class players, Crenshaw may well be the best putter of recent times, but Tom Watson commands a much higher profile on the greens. This stems from his record as the dominant force on the US Tour for several years and the holder of the best record in major championships over that period. With five British Opens, one US Open and two US Masters under his belt, he easily qualifies for a place high up in the all-time rankings.

It is said that, early in his career, Watson had a passion to play perfect golf: to hit all the fairways and greens in regulation strokes. In the end, the real world caught up with him, realizing that this was impossible, he proceeded to work, just as single-mindedly, on his short game. How well he succeeded is revealed by a body of opinion once held among his fellow professionals that, if all the players missed all the greens, then Tom Watson would be the only possible winner. Quite simply, the best, from close to the greens or on them.

Television cameras, with their concentration on putting, put Tom's skills under a ruthless spotlight. He is unusual in that his grip on the putter is firmer than most, an exception which doesn't disprove the general rule. Mentally a reincarnation of the young Arnold Palmer, he really believed that he could make every putt, realizing that a sure way to fail in that is to fall short of the hole. Tom always 'gave the hole a chance', having confidence that he could hole those return putts from, let's say, five feet or so. Alas, he's far more tentative today.

That's one feature of his game which teaches a valuable lesson. Another is his belief that a constant angle of the left elbow is vital – another moving part which can be eliminated, just like the necessity to avoid breaking the wrists.

The short but challenging, 7th hole at Pebble Beach, California.

While many links courses are often relatively flat, their greens can be deceptively undulating.

You can analyze that by trying out a putting stroke for yourself. Experiment by allowing your elbow to change position, and also by maintaining the same angle. It won't be difficult to sense the very different qualities of strike you obtain if you let the elbow flex, as you try meeting the ball with the clubhead descending sometimes, and on the rise at others. Actually, the effect is much the same as if you have allowed the wrists to flex.

Tom Watson once gave a memorable demonstration of this during a television programme. With all the aplomb in the world, he rattled in a series of medium-length putts while retaining a constant left elbow, and then showed how inconsistent results became when he allowed it to flex. What was really memorable was the way he knocked in that sequence with total ease and nonchalance. Most of us would be happy to have holed just one of them!

It isn't as difficult as you may think to keep that elbow angle constant. All you need do is feel that your back-and-through movement is coming from the joint of the arms with the shoulders. It doesn't matter much what that elbow angle is, whether you start with your elbow fairly straight as Ben Crenshaw does, or bent as in the Tom Watson method. What does matter is that the amount of bend remains constant throughout your putting stroke.

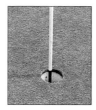

# PUTTING – THE SHORT AND THE LONG OF IT

I t's often been said that putting is a 'game within a game'. The idea is that wholly different skills are necessary on the green than are needed for the long game; that a star golfer must be able to propel the ball for 300 yards using a swing that travels at over 100 mph, but must also consistently get the ball into the hole from three feet.

I would go further. For me, short putting is a very different game from long putting. Once you are close to the

You must hole the short ones.

Toppling in from the side.

Don't try knocking them in one-handed.

Or reaching over the hole for a tap-in – this can happen and often does.

Using clubs to check body alignment to target line.

hole, there is relatively little need for feel, and the problem is fundamentally a simple one. All you need do is find a method which consistently moves the ball along your chosen line, into the hole, looming there, almost under your nose.

Sounds simple doesn't it? A child could do it, and many can – when it doesn't matter.

Some golfers don't need to change the mechanical method that experience has provided for them, when they reach the green. Others do. To recap some of the ground we've covered before, it may help to grip the club more firmly, giving you the feeling that you are striking more definitely, and also helping you to avoid the blade of your putter meeting the ball when open or closed.

That blade must be square with your target line. If you are not allowing for any borrow, imagine your putter head is sitting on one of a pair of parallel lines, the other running across the middle of the hole.

Don't just aim at the hole – that's much too vague. Pick a spot on the front or rear lip, according to taste, and aim at that. Presenting yourself with a tiny target forces you to be more precise.

You do need to feel the strength of your stroke, even though, on a flat putt, there is little chance of your finishing disastrously far past the hole. Many short putts are missed when the player simply 'forgets' to hit the ball hard enough. He's thinking solely of direction, and finds it all too easy to come up six inches short on a 12-inch putt.

There is another point worth remembering, too. You'll recall that, in an earlier chapter, I have stressed the advantages of 'straightening out' curving short putts by hitting firmly. This doesn't apply significantly on flat putts, although a minute spike mark, or even the lie of the grass, may divert a slowly moving ball. That consideration apart, make your own decision about whether you feel happier when striking your putts crisply. If you decide you are, then you'll find yourself better served by striking firmly at the back of the hole.

Remember, also, that you need only be slightly off line for your ball to spin away from the edge of the hole. However, this isn't the case if your ball is moving very slowly. Here, you have three chances of the putt dropping: over the front lip, or from either side. And they can occasionally drop in from the back as well.

It's fatally easy to be careless with very short putts. Ask Hale Irwin, who has reason to know. He won the 1990 US Open after a vast putt across the 72nd green got him into the play-off, and a straightforward eight-footer settled things for him on the 91st. Yet seven years earlier, he had failed to tie for the 1983 British Open through a moment of sheer

**ABOVE LEFT AND RIGHT:** Plumb-bobbing. Hold your putter shaft vertically. If there's a side-slope between you and the hole, the theory is that the slope will show up as an angle of more or less than 90 degrees.

carelessness. His ball lay right on the lip of the hole, and he leaned over to tap it in nonchalantly.

And then missed the ball altogether.

So – don't take an age over it, but no matter how short the putt, do settle yourself into your normal putting stance, and make your normal stroke. No putting on the walk. No careless pushes or pulls.

*Feel* is what long putting is all about. Feel for distance, feel for the pace of the green, feel in your putting stroke. Even your club pro can only really help you with your basic method. The rest is down to experience.

Tournament players take a great deal of time pacing out their putts, examining the line from behind the ball and from either side. But I take leave to wonder if it really does them any good. I suspect that, most of the time, they are only confirming the impressions they got when they first walked on to the green.

Having said that, some things really are worth taking a look at, especially near the hole, when your ball will be travelling slowly and therefore most likely to deviate.

If the grain of the grass is against your putt, your chances of finishing short of the hole are increased. If the

**LEFT AND RIGHT:** Good feel for distance here. The ball is almost dead.

**RIGHT TO LEFT, TOP TO BOTTOM:** From a few feet away, closer still and finally, a look at how the hole is cut.

grain is away from you, you should be more concerned with making sure you're not likely to end up a long way past the hole. Around the hole itself, the grass is more likely to be flattened and worn. This may prevent your ball from stopping as quickly as a casual glance at the hole from a distance might have suggested.

A little experience will soon teach you about the effect of the putting surface on the distance your ball travels. You can hardly fail to notice, for example, that a close-cut surface has quite different characteristics from one showing a full day's growth.

Moisture, or lack of it, can also bring dramatic changes. Compare the behavior of a burned-brown summer green with that of the same area during the thick, lush growing season. You'll also soon begin to notice the difference between an area of grass which has been shaded from the sun all day and one which has been in the sun all day.

These factors also need to be considered when there is a question of borrow rather than strength. Simply, there is more borrow when the surface is fast than when it is slow.

Looking at the hole.

These pine needles could deflect a putt, so move any debris on the line of your putt.

**LEFT:** When a green is close to a lake, it may putt slower on the side nearest the water.

Once you've made your judgements of pace and line, that information has to be translated to your putting stroke. In fact, line is of lesser importance unless there is severe borrow. On a 20-yard putt you are far more likely to be five yards long or short than you are to be five yards wide. Judgement of strength, and how to produce that exactly in your putting stroke, is therefore more vital than judgement of direction. That will largely take care of itself, assuming you have the basics right.

**ABOVE AND RIGHT:** How the grass has been cut affects the pace of a putt. When it's shiny you are with the cut, and pace will be quicker. It's a slower putt and against the grain when the grass looks darker. Putting across the line of cut makes little difference.

**ABOVE:** A parched summer green.

**TOP AND ABOVE:** After a day's growth, the grain produced by cutting has gone.

This is where the putter with a light grip comes into his or her own. No one can be successful in long putting unless the muscles of the arms remain relaxed, although some players would disagree as far as short putts are concerned.

Some golfers – Tom Watson, for example, who seems to give his putts a little punch with his lower arms – like to think that the very small amount of power needed is provided by the forearms. If you have a rather pendulum motion with the arms, however, try to feel the strength needed for the putt with the upper arm, muscles relaxed yet active.

Finding the sweet spot and exact striking are equally important. You can hit a short putt very poorly and still find the hole, but disaster is certain from long range. Tests using machines prove that, on a 60-foot putt, a ball struck one inch away from the sweet spot will finish 15 feet short of the hole. Reduce that error to a half-inch and you'll still be five feet short, with a three-putt looming.

It's more difficult to judge the line when shade and sunlight alternate on a green.

If part of a green has been in the shade, it will putt more slowly.

The same machine was used to compare strength and correct performance of actual strokes. Tournament professionals putted against it over 60 feet. The pro's holed just 3% of their shots. Even the 'perfect' machine only managed 20% – but invariably got the ball close to the hole.

The lessons are clear as regards long putting. A green isn't a snooker or pool table. It changes second by second, depending how each blade of grass is lying at the time. Holing out from a distance is, therefore, always something of a fluke.

Your approach for all those putts which lie between the obviously long, and the clearly short, should be the same as for long ones. From, say, 20 feet, tournament pro's still miss nine times out of ten (even the machine only managed 50%).

Once more, the lesson is that you should concentrate on getting the distance right and let nature take care of the line. Your target should be to get the ball close. *Feel* the distance and concentrate on a pure strike, rather than try to 'will' the ball along your imagined line into the hole.

**TOP LEFT, RIGHT AND ABOVE:** This putt is straight at the hole – but well short.

**ABOVE:** The putter can be your friend from unlikely positions – if you can develop feel for the run of the ball.

**LEFT:** Judging a slope like this takes extreme talent (St Andrews).

**ABOVE AND RIGHT:** Good feel for distance here.

## SHORT OR LONG BACKSWING?

Here, you need to use your personal feel for the ball to arrive at an acceptable compromise. Backswing too short, and you'll find yourself forcing your putter head at the ball, because you haven't allowed yourself enough swing to produce the necessary amount of momentum. Too long and a whole new set of problems appear.

To start with, the more distance the club has to travel, the more chances there are of wavering or wandering off line. Mentally, you are also far more likely to feel doubts as your club moves back to the ball, a condition which often leads to your slowing the club down and hitting the ball less firmly than required.

In fact, there aren't really any firm rules to follow, although some pundits have tried to simplify things by

Huge slopes can be very difficult to judge (St Andrews).

An extremely difficult putt if your approach is past the hole.

stating how far back you should swing for a putt of – say –
30 feet as opposed to one of 20 feet. If you think about it, this
is absolute nonsense, because it makes no allowance for the
pace of the greens. That particular factor is a matter of
experience; of playing and practicing on all varieties of
putting surface.

The only answer is to experiment until your backswing
is a matter that doesn't require thought, becomes automatic,
and works for you.

## SHORT OR LONG
## FOLLOW-THROUGH?

The face of your putter is in contact with the ball for a tiny
fraction of a second, and this is true whether you jab at the
ball or putt with a smooth, flowing stroke and a relaxed
follow-through. So everything depends on what kind of action
gives you best results.

I have mentioned Gary Player as a great putter with a
'jabbing' action. It's always worked for him, and still does,
over a career of 30 years or more. Nevertheless, he once won
the US Masters after his wife suggested he revert to a
smoother stroke which had served him well at an earlier stage
in his development. He used it for a while, but eventually
returned to the tried and true method which he trusted more.

**LEFT AND RIGHT:** This is better. A confident
putter aims to be past the hole.

# CHAPTER EIGHTEEN

# SPIN, MIND AND TWITCHES

In theory, jabbing down on the ball imparts backspin, and hitting it on the up results in topspin. Unfortunately, things aren't quite as simple as that.

Years ago, many golfers liked to use a putter with loft: greens weren't so smooth and consistent as today, and a degree of loft made the ball travel in the air for a short distance, so that the ball was well on its way before being checked or deflected for the first time.

With an elevated green, it can pay to putt your ball short, particularly when the ground is hard and dry.

Bobby Jones' famous putter, 'Calamity Jane', with which he achieved most of his successes, had a loft of some eight degrees, much the same as a rather straight-faced driver of today. 'Calamity', and her sisters, almost certainly gave some backspin, not an advantage in putting, although that early travel off the ground could be useful on poor winter greens.

During medium or long putts, the ball travels off the ground for a short distance (depending on the length of the shot), then skids for a while, before rolling for the rest of its journey.

It is even possible to apply cut or hook spin to a putt. Old-time players liked to cut the ball into a right-to-left slope, believing that this kept the ball on line, just as if they were hitting a wood or iron into a right-to-left wind. However, the spin only lasts for a very short time, for that period when the ball is travelling in the air, or skidding. After that, the ball's forward momentum rapidly removes any sidespin.

**TOP LEFT AND RIGHT, AND ABOVE:** Every putt is *hit* straight, even though this one *travelled* left to right.

The ball is skidding here. You can see from its shadow that the ball is off the putting surface.

The putter on the right is favored by players who are struck down with the 'yips' – that inability to hit the ball. The extension of the putter is rested against the player's chin and held with one hand. The other hand does the work.

**LEFT:** Although the fairway is brown, there's nothing wrong with this putting surface.

**ABOVE AND OPPOSITE:** You must get the medium-length putts stone dead.

# 'YOU PUTT INSIDE YOUR MIND'

At the peak of Tony Jacklin's career, which covered the years 1968–73, his fellow professionals thought him nearly infallible in the vital three-to-four-foot range. For the rest, he was a 'streak' putter. There were days when he couldn't go wrong, and others when he came well down from the heights.

Those short putts are a matter of technique and confidence. If you *know* you're going to hit them straight from short range, then you'll hole the lot – and much the same is true when you are just a few feet further away, say, up to about eight feet.

Tony lost all certainty. He felt he had to hit his approach shots very close indeed to give him birdies. Similarly, he felt he had to get his long putts very close to avoid three-putting.

There were still the 'golden days' when the battle 'inside your mind' was won. Alas, they didn't come frequently enough to keep Tony Jacklin at the top of the tree.

The pressures of tournament golf are very great, and those of a major championship even greater. After all, a man is playing for his livelihood, wealth, even a kind of immortality, but the club golfer doesn't live in an entirely different world. It is often very important for them, too, to play well, to win matches and competitions.

The importance of an event is relative, and it is that importance which applies the pressure. Regarding it all as unimportant, even treating it casually, doesn't help. And there has to be a balance between producing as good a performance as possible, with maximum concentration, and collapsing under the strain.

It isn't easy. You have to divorce yourself from the occasion – say, going for a good score in a strokeplay competition – and think only of the putt you are facing.

The buzzing of the flies, your partner's infuriating habit of shuffling their feet, any extraneous distraction – they're all irrelevant. So are thoughts about what a disaster it will be if you fail to get this 12-footer stone dead, and miss the next one.

No. It isn't easy, but it has to be done. Concentrate on the job in hand, and ignore everything else.

## LIVING WITH A TWITCH

Call it a 'twitch', 'the yips', 'jerks' or whatever: 'Once you've had 'em, you've got 'em.' That was the opinion of Henry Longhurst, the best golf writer of modern times.

If you haven't a clue what I'm talking about, then perhaps you shouldn't read any further. However, I've never heard of a case of this dreaded disease incurred by simply reading about it, so it's probably safe to continue.

The twitch is a muscular spasm of hands or arms which can occur during the putting stroke. At best, it means a poor ball strike: at worst, your putter can propel the ball clean off the green.

Many great players have suffered, and many have been forced out of competitive golf. In fact, more have left the game this way than through the sheer decline of physical powers in the long game.

I remember talking to ABC and BBC golf commentator Peter Alliss about the dreaded scourge. Peter was a top British star in the 1950s and 60s, and although still an automatic choice for Ryder Cup teams, retired from tournament play in 1969.

'You know,' he said, 'I can even be putting casually at a chair leg, but if I say to myself, "this is for real", I'm likely to twitch it.'

Bernhard Langer provides a much better-known example. Twitching usually seems to arise after years of tournament play, but Bernhard's case wasn't like that. He twitched as a teenager, and has had to endure severe attacks ever since. If anyone should know a cure, he should.

Like all other sufferers, Langer never has found a permanent remedy, but he has learned to live with it well enough to win a Masters, and a host of other titles throughout the world.

Bernhard's twitch seems to occur in the left wrist. He has learned to live with it in three distinct phases, and in three different ways. Early in the 80s he found a putter which he really liked, the twitch disappeared, and almost overnight he became one of the best putters on the European Tour. Sam Snead had the same experience in the 1940s.

For Langer, the magic putter failed after a couple of years or so. His next solution was to play short putts with left hand below right, reverting to his normal reverse overlap for the longer ones. It's highly unusual to change grips in this way, and many people wondered how he decided which grip to use. Did he change over at a certain distance from the hole? Not a bit of it. The normally methodical German was more instinctive than that. He just changed over 'when it felt right'.

In 1988 that cure failed too, to such an extent that he took five putts on one green during the 1988 Open. After long experimentation, he arrived at a truly strange grip. The left

**LEFT:** A putting green will nearly always slope towards water, even if very slightly.

hand remained below the right, but he now held his left forearm with the fingers of his right hand, while the palm helped support the putter. In effect, if a nervous spasm was causing his left wrist to twitch, then his new grip made the club shaft into a splint. Bernhard Langer was on his way once more.

I'm not suggesting that Langer's splint technique is an answer to problems for the golfer at club level, but if you are afflicted, then there are advantages to making changes, even quite minor ones.

Identify, as closely as possible, where that tremor is. Then change your stroke so as to take that troublesome area out of it.

Many club golfers don't realize that they have a tremor. It occurs only occasionally, for example, when faced with an important putt, downhill with a left-to-right break. The shorter the putt, the worse the twitch, because the shorter the shot, the more shame-making it is to miss.

If such a golfer misses, they put the blame on lack of concentration, misjudgement of line, looking up too quickly and any other reason they can think of. But it's really all an excuse. Anything to avoid the admission that they have that fatal, nervous spasm.

The practice green, obviously feeling the effect of a hot dry summer. In such conditions the greens play faster than normal.

# PUTTING FROM OFF THE GREEN

Remember that the putter isn't restricted to the putting surface. Let's look at an extreme example.

Once upon a time, two good young players arrived at the tee of a par 3 in a friendly practice round. One, the club champion incidentally, hit a 6-iron to about 10 feet and stood aside. His playing companion then started to debate about which club he should use. Was it a hard 6-iron for him, or perhaps a more relaxed 5-iron? Or, because the ground was

If your ball lands on the wrong half of a double green, you could be faced with a very long putt.

firm, perhaps he ought to pitch well short of the green and let the ball run on? That might be an 8-iron shot.

'Look,' said the club champion, 'if you're a real golfer, you ought to be able to play this 160-yard hole with just about any club in the bag. Play a running punch shot with a 4-iron, hit a high fade with a wood, hood a wedge. You can even play it with a putter.'

With these final words, he snatched his blade putter out of his bag and, without a glance towards the green, swung.

Cleanly struck, the ball flew off on line for the gap between two bunkers guarding the front left and right of the green. With its low trajectory, it pitched well short of the green but held its line and ran towards the flag. And on. And on. And in.

A hole in one is as good a way as any to prove one's point. His companion has, however, been trying to get his own hole in one with a putter from time to time ever since. Without success.

So I'm not suggesting that a putter is often going to be the best club selection for a shot of 160 yards.

But it can come into play far more often than you might think. We are too inclined to think of golf as a game played by the air route. We dream of shots that soar upwards and plummet down at the flag, bounce once and come to a stop, stone dead by the holeside. There seems to be less glory – some think it's almost cheating – to bumble the ball along the ground. So here are some situations when the putter can give you a good result when it's not the conventional choice of club.

## FROM THE FRINGE

I must admit that quite a few golfers do believe that putting from the fringe of the green is socially and morally acceptable, even if chipping is 'the proper golf shot'. Unless you are a very good chipper of the ball, the chances are you'll get a better average result using your putter. Put it to the test in practice and notice these things in particular. From say 10 yards or so, you'll probably feel reasonably satisfied if you chip to 2 yards. Yet when you get exactly that result with your putter, you'll probably feel you've made a bad putt. If those are your feelings, the messages are obvious. For you, the putter is an easier club to use in this situation. So use it.

**RIGHT:** A well-protected two-tier green.

Ian Woosnam about to take on a tricky putt.

## FROM A GREENSIDE BUNKER

To putt successfully from a bunker, three factors must be in your favor.

(1)   There must be no front lip at all on the bunker to stop or divert your ball.

(2)   The sand must be firm rather than soft and fluffy. If it's soft, your ball won't roll freely over the surface but will stop quickly. The ideal time to use a putter is when the sand is wet after rain or as a result of the greens being watered.

(3)   You must have a clean lie – that is, the ball must be entirely, or almost entirely, above the sand. Once it is down just a little, you may succeed in moving the ball out of the bunker but judgement of how firmly to strike is impossible.

## IN A BIG WIND

The higher your golf ball flies, the more it is affected by the wind. This, of course, applies just as much when you're near the green as for long shots. The way to keep it as low as possible is by using your putter. Whether the wind is behind you or in your face makes little difference.

It will still affect how far your ball runs, but far less so than if you play a high pitch. The difference is so great, in fact, that you need make little allowance for it át all.

# THE TEXAS WEDGE

Texas is famous for producing golfers who know how to play in strong winds. If they don't learn, they might as well give up the game. This is true also of golfers who play on seaside links, high moors and heathlands. You seldom encounter a totally still day.

So what is this wedge? A putter. The nickname came about when other American golfers noticed how often Texans used their putters from well short of the green – from normal wedge distance in fact. This can be up to 120 yards but it would probably be foolhardy to use a putter from more than 50 yards from the green.

Texans and other golfers don't confine use of the putter from long range only to windy weather. They also use the club when they feel they are going to get a better result than when playing a pitch shot.

The key point to bear in mind is that the putter is simply the easiest club to use. The shaft is short, which means that your hands are nearer the ball than with any other club. That makes a golf stroke just that little bit easier. The lack of loft also makes a consistent result from a given impact speed much more attainable.

Many golfers never attempt to use the putter from long range. As I mentioned earlier, there is a strong feeling that 'it isn't golf' and that you look silly if you putt and finish either

**TOP, ABOVE AND LEFT:** Using a putter from off the green can produce more accurate results than those afforded by a lofted club.

many yards short of the green or way through the back. But this can happen with other clubs as well.

Experience is necessary. In the first place, you are hitting the ball much harder than normal. From being an always gentle stroke, the putt becomes quite firm. I don't think you can expect to get reasonable results if you try the shot every once in a while.

Practice, and on-course experience, will soon teach you a lot about how the ball runs, even over quite uneven ground. You can even putt over semi-rough, provided it isn't close-knitted.

Remember, earlier golfers must have consistently used their putters once they were near the greens. Why? Well, even though they did have lofted woods, pitching clubs as such didn't exist. So they putted instead. What irons they had were really intended for escaping trouble – bunkers, rough and ruts (no relief in far-off days!). Otherwise, a lofted wood, such as the baffy, was the club to pitch with and you wouldn't think of using it for anything under 80 yards.

The Texas wedge can be used over both wet and dry ground. Many prefer to use the shot only when the ground is dry and firm – when it's a little more like a putting green.

However, the shot can be equally, perhaps more, effective in the wet. The little bumps your ball strikes will be softer and divert your long putt less. The greens will also be considerably slower, which means less likelihood of a clumsy long putt racing through over a fast dry putting surface.

# PUTTING OVER SEVERE UNDULATIONS

This time your ball is quite close to the green but with a bank between you and the hole, with the flag set close to that bank. This is the situation when you'll often hear a television commentator at a tournament say, 'He hasn't got much green to work with.' The commentator means that the golfer playing, for example, a short pitch shot, must be very precise. Their ball must only just clear the bank and reach the putting surface since the hole is only a very few yards onto the green.

In this case, the experienced golfer may think the putt is the percentage shot. As long as the grass is closely mown, it may well work better.

It all depends on how you see it and where your skills lie. Mark Calcavecchia, then British Open champion, was playing the Old Course at St Andrews in the Dunhill Cup in 1989.

**LEFT:** Of course, putting can be the least of your problems!

**ABOVE AND RIGHT:** You often get a better result when putting, rather than chipping, from the fringe of the green.

The Old Course has many double greens, with the result that a player can be on undulating surfaces, perhaps 50 yards further away from the hole than they are accustomed to.

Calcavecchia certainly wasn't used to it. He aroused quite a storm amongst both St Andreans and the press by wedging to the hole instead. Divots flew from the sacred turf. Calcavecchia repaired the damage on both occasions he tried the shot with exemplary care, but it still didn't satisfy onlookers.

Under the rules of golf he was fully entitled to wedge away on the greens to his heart's content, though I suspect many golfers wouldn't have known this. Mark later said that he just wasn't used to putting from such great distances and felt he had no chance of getting his ball close – but he was used to short wedge shots.

Ironically, both the Calcavecchia wedge shots were poor. He would almost certainly have done better with his putter. And that's the lesson of my story.

# PRACTICE ROUTINES

The first thing to bear in mind is that your golf club practice green is probably nothing like the ones you'll encounter out on the course. It may not have been constructed in the same way, not cut to the same rhythm, and it isn't likely that any consistent attempt has been made to ensure that it plays at the same speed as the others.

This is a point you should certainly take into consideration, especially if you decide to take a few putts before an important round. It's preferable to limit your long-putt practice to getting the feel of your putting stroke, and making sure that your strike is in good order. There's little

Putting becomes a lot easier if you can put your approach shot onto the right tier of the green!

Many prefer to aim at the hole . . .

. . . but sometimes there's no need. Concentrate on your stroke and ball strike.

point in hitting a lot of putts to distant targets as if you were playing the actual course.

Short putting, on the other hand, won't do you much harm, because feel for pace is less important. The approach you use will depend on your own mental make-up. If missing a few very short ones is likely to damage your confidence, then try to be casual about the whole thing; concentrate on a good putting stroke and exact striking rather than trying to sink every putt. There's no real need even to aim at the hole.

On the other hand, it might suit your psychology best to pretend it's all for real. In that case, take care over every putt, telling yourself, 'It's this one for the championship.' Concentrate on short putts and maintain some method.

It can boost your confidence to hole a few from very short range, and then gradually move further away: if you miss one – start over.

But don't be content to keep putting along the same line. It's better to avoid that sort of sheer mechanical repetition by moving around the hole and *forcing* yourself to think about every putt.

And finally – don't spend too long on the green. Remember, you're going to be driving off from the first tee soon, and you don't want to cramp your style for that vital moment!

## GENERAL PUTTING PRACTICE

Concentrate, first of all, on checking over your putting stroke, something which can be done at home, or even at work.

Set up close to a wall, playing parallel to it. If your putter head makes contact with the wall when you are making your stroke, then you have some valuable information.

If you hit it on your backswing – that's bad news. It tells you that you aren't taking your club straight back, let alone along the preferable slightly-inside trajectory. If that kind of take-away persists, then you're going to be cutting across the ball.

Alternatively, you can lay another club down, and proceed as before, using the shaft as an indication of basic faults in your stroke. When you are satisfied that your stroke mechanics are in working order, you can set it the task of actually sinking putts.

Practice putting from different directions.

The 18th at St Andrews.

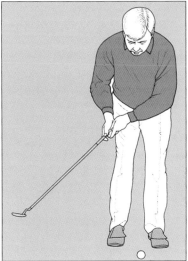

No wrist break in the putting stroke.

**TOP AND ABOVE:** Think about why you missed. Using just one ball can make each putt seem more important – especially if you don't like too much walking.

Don't indulge in long practice sessions, but make your practice intensive, and as real as you can. Avoid aimlessly and quickly striking a succession of putts, whether long or short. Tell yourself that each putt matters, and after each putt, pause to think out why you succeeded or failed that time.

It's a good idea not to use too many balls, and a better one to make your practice as competitive as possible. One way of doing this is to use two balls, imagining you have a match on – Curtis Strange against Nick Faldo, for example.

Better still, ask a real-life opponent to join in. Play for enough money to hurt, but not to wound – although Lee Trevino once said that real pressure is playing for $5 when you haven't got $5.

Who knows? You might become another George Low.

He was a US tournament player who found that he wasn't really good enough to make a living at it, even though he was outstanding on the greens. Accordingly, he took to hanging around the practice greens, playing all-comers for money.

It paid off a lot better than tournament golf.

# RULES AND GOLF COURSE BEHAVIOR

The first action a player should take is to repair their pitch mark. This is probably best done with the well-known fork-like tool. Acceptable substitutes include a tee peg or pocket knife. The aim is to lift out the indentation your ball has made. There will always be one, except when the greens are very hard or if you've played only a short shot in. If you cannot find your mark, repair one or more others instead. You'll then be a saint where so many other golfers are sinners. When you've lifted the turf, gently tamp it down flat with the sole of your putter. Don't use your feet; you'll merely replace one kind of damage with another – spike marks.

All this can, and should, be done quickly: golf can become agonizingly slow once players reach the putting surface. Let's treat this aspect of behavior towards your fellow golfers first (the people waiting behind you).

Quickly decide who is furthest from the hole and is therefore first to putt. An exception would be if one of our imaginary fourball is in a bunker. He or she should play first, even though they may well be nearest the hole. The player may have to swing the club quite fast if they have a buried lie and a bad shot would mean the ball whizzes across the green. This change in the normal order of play is simply for safety reasons.

One of the non-putters should be stationed at the flagstick and either attend it or take it out, depending upon what they are asked to do. While this is done, they shouldn't either stand too close to the hole or on the line of any other player's putt; as this creates spike marks.

While anyone is putting, the other players should stand still, not either immediately behind or beyond the line of putt. This is to avoid distracting the putter. They should also be careful to make no noise. Also be careful not to cast a shadow on or near the line of putt.

Each player, when walking to the putting position, should have the line of putt of the other players in mind. Either walk around this line or take a stride over.

Players will often be asked to, or choose to, mark their balls on the green. The purposes are several: to avoid their being struck by another ball; to remove them as a distraction when there is only an outside chance of their being struck; to clean them; to examine them for suspected damage and to set the ball down in a position the player finds useful. (Many like the writing to run horizontally across the equator of the ball; some might like the writing, still central, to run vertically; others might prefer to set the number exactly in the centre with the idea of bringing the sweet spot of the putter exactly into contact with this number.)

Much of this is a matter of personal taste. How you mark the ball isn't. This should be set down snugly behind the ball – not between ball and hole. Use a small coin or one of the variety of small discs with a spike.

Occasionally, your marker may be on, or near to, someone's putting line. You will then be asked to move your marker. There is a correct way of doing this. With the ball in place, measure a putterhead's distance away, pick up the ball, set it down against the toe of your putter and then re-mark the ball. Carry on in the same way if you are asked to move further.

All this shouldn't be allowed to take your ball either nearer or further away from the hole, so aim at some convenient point at right angles.

Alas, not a few golfers over the years have used marking their ball to provide opportunities to get it just a little nearer the hole. While there is no significant advantage in doing this on the tee (by playing from an inch or so in front of the tee markers), this can be very different on the green. Here, a couple of inches or so can have a great effect on the golfer's confidence. To him or her, an 18 inch putt may be the easiest thing to hole successfully. Doubts may seep in at 20 inches.

Professionals have been caught out cheating when marking their golf balls on the green and have been banned from the game.

Greens are the most delicate surfaces on the golf course. So far, by repairing pitch marks, we've done one job. If you are using a trolley or cart, this obviously should not be taken onto the putting surface, but you must also avoid the closely mown surrounds. At one time, golfers used to place their bags carefully on the greens, but this is frowned upon today. Instead, lay them down on the surrounds or rougher ground somewhere near your route to the next tee, to save time later on.

Try to avoid excessive marking of the putting surface with your feet. This can happen when a player, for example, twists about in mental agony when a putt narrowly misses. If you do transgress, repair the damage before you leave the green.

You can also cause damage with your putter, and that's aside from banging it on the turf in fury! Don't thrust it into the hole after putting with the aim of flicking the ball out. This can scar the edge of the hole. Don't lean heavily on your putter at any time and, when retrieving your ball from the hole, don't lean on it to help keep your balance.
You shouldn't really need a prop for this simple act – though most professionals seem to!

When you arrive on the green, your preparations for putting should be made as quickly as your temperament allows. There's no excuse for any delay once you've completed play. Your clubs should be on your route to the next tee (not abandoned at the front of the green, where you remain in range as you collect your clubs and delay the following games). Get moving!

Though not so much as teeing grounds, putting greens are well defined, although by no means regular in shape. The rules that govern play on the greens are also simpler than for play on the rest of a golf course.

You can remove all loose impediments on the green. This also includes any under your ball where you simply mark, lift, remove the offending item and replace your ball. Beware, however, of being accused of testing the surface of the green.
For instance, brushing the putting surface with your fingers or palm could well enable you to decide the grain of the grass and is not allowed. Avoid offending by sweeping away such impediments as leaves or pine needles with the back of your hand or putter and lift them individually if there are not too many.

Remember that you, your caddie or partner can help you decide where to aim your putt, but no one may make a mark and may only point, not lay a finger on the ground.

If you strike another ball, this means a penalty (different for stroke and match play) and striking the flag incurs a two-stroke penalty if you are on the putting surface rather than the fringe.

Remember there are also rules about how you stand to the ball. Years ago, golfers who developed a putting twitch found that a croquet stroke brought a cure. They acquired a mallet-like putter

and stood astride the line, the ball between the legs. The club was held at the top with the left hand and the strike came from the right hand, well down the shaft. Sam Snead was a great player who found this method brought relief from his twitches on the greens. Perhaps unkindly, golf's authorities banned the method. Although it is unlikely to affect you, remember that leaning over the hole, when you've sent a short putt a very few inches past, usually means that you will have a foot on either side of the line – and have broken the rule.

'The Blackheath Golfer', a 1778 engraving by Lemuel Abbott. It is the earliest depiction of an English golfer, believed to be William Innes, captain of the Blackheath Club at the time.

**ABOVE:** As this is a practice bunker it is less frequently raked, so you have more chance to practice your recovery shots.

# TROUBLE SHOOTING

# INTRODUCTION

Golf is a cross-country game. Intended playing areas may be superbly maintained, but most of the course consists of relatively natural terrain when compared with the surfaces on which – say – tennis or bowls are played.

This means that even a perfect shot can result in difficulties (the lie of the ball, for example), and if a shot is less than perfect, we can expect to be, and very often are, in real trouble.

Some of those difficulties, such as bunkers and artificial water, are placed for precisely that purpose by the course architect – to punish a golfer for his mistakes. Others are simply the result of playing over natural ground. The situations one can find there are often, perhaps even usually, more difficult to play from than any bunker.

This book aims to cover all the trouble shots a golfer may expect to play, not just in one round, but throughout the golfing year. You can't expect to play brilliant recoveries from every predicament, but I hope you'll find at least partial solutions in these pages. That's about all we can expect in trouble shooting country.

**ABOVE:** Natural linksland.

# IN SAND

Most club golfers choose clubs by the set of a dozen or so. Some, perhaps a little more thoughtful, may go so far as separating the woods from the irons and choose each category separately.

Professionals have a very different approach. The next time you are at a tournament, see if you can get a look in the pros' bags, especially those of the less-famous players. If you manage it, you are likely to see a tremendous variety of makes and models, with the only approach to uniformity appearing in the range of irons, from about 7 to 3. Every other one is likely to be regarded as a specialist club.

Every golfer selects a putter as an individual item, even if there are dozens in the collection, but the pro is out to find just that driver, 1-iron, fairway wood, couple of wedges and especially the sand iron which he eventually decides best suits his swing and his methods.

While the driver probably heads the priority list, the sand iron gets as much attention as any other.

Why is this?

## BUNKERS – CHOOSING A SAND IRON

Top professionals miss a lot of greens, as a glance at the statistics published by both the US and European Tours will reveal. They show that even the best player in the 'greens in regulation' category – which means a par 3 in one, a par 4 in two and a par 5 in three – fails about 25 per cent of the time. But he doesn't miss any of them by much. So where does he finish? In the greenside bunkers, of course.

He then becomes a far more impressive golfer. One who gets down in two more than 60 per cent of the time.

No wonder the pros consider the sand iron so important and why they spend so much time selecting just the right club. You don't need to go to extremes, but it's well worth while for you to give the matter your keen consideration. You certainly shouldn't discard a good sand iron when changing a set of irons.

So just what makes a good sand iron? Let's take the main desirable characteristics first.

The most important thing to consider is the sole, and here the sand iron differs considerably from the other irons. Here, it takes the form of a heavy flange which is higher at the leading edge than the trailing edge, and it is that trailing edge which helps prevent your clubhead from digging into the sand, and encourages it to ride through instead.

This kind of club was invented by Gene Sarazen in 1931. He didn't consider himself a good sand player, and experimented with soldering lead to the sole of an iron until he had developed that higher trailing edge which enabled him to coast the clubhead through sand rather than dig down into it. The following year, Gene won both the US and British Opens and gave much of the credit to his new invention. Indeed, he had revolutionised bunker play by making the normal 'splash' shot much easier for the average player. He also enabled the very good ones to think in terms of getting much closer to the hole, or even holing out. Because of this good players no longer had to be content with simply getting out of the bunker to anywhere on the green.

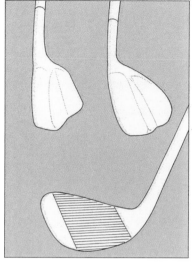

A selection of irons, with a 9-iron top left and a sand iron top right

**ABOVE:** Two sand irons, with the necessary higher trailing edge.

The club you choose should also be heavy. This means you really feel the clubhead throughout your swing, and can play your sand shots with less force.

In later years, people have tried to improve the sand iron. At least one of these so-called 'improvements' should be avoided.

At first sight, it would seem an obvious advantage to have a club which will do two jobs: get you out of bunkers and also be useful for pitching, the sand iron having considerably more loft than the wedge. Hence the development of the so-called 'dual purpose' sand irons.

However, the trailing edge of the sand iron makes it much more difficult to pitch with. There is always the danger that the rear edge will come into contact with the turf first, and cause the club to bounce, resulting in a thinned shot as your leading edge catches the ball around the equator.

The obvious solution was to reduce the height of the trailing edge. Certainly, you have a far better pitching club, but it doesn't work nearly as well in the sand.

So be on the lookout for any club which claims to do both jobs, and having found it – ignore it completely. It's far better to invest in a second wedge for pitching, and you really do need that high trailing edge for sand play.

Just how high the trailing edge should be depends on where you play most of your golf. Fine, soft sand demands a high trailing edge, and the actual height needed diminishes as the sand becomes coarser. Many professionals travel with two sand irons and decide which one to use when they've had a look at the bunkers.

You can't really know how well a sand iron will suit you until you try it out. You can experiment with used clubs from your pro, or borrow a few from fellow golfers until you decide on the right one. But please don't blindly accept the sand iron which comes with a new set of clubs. At least, inspect it to see if it follows the guidelines.

**RIGHT:** This sequence illustrates a normal splash shot. Note the relaxed address position and the fairly full backswing.

ABOVE: How the sand explodes the ball out.

# GREENSIDE BUNKERS

The first consideration here is the lie of the ball. Let's start with the most simple shot; when the ball is lying cleanly, only the very bottom of it being below the surface.

Even a journeyman pro is delighted to be confronted by this shot. True – he'd rather be putting, but he will probably be much more confident of getting close to the flag from sand than from a grass lie. This contrasts sharply with the attitude of a club golfer who lacks confidence in his sand play: he will be preoccupied with how to get out, and doubtful if he can manage it at all, never mind getting close to the hole.

'Just getting out' is, in fact, the simplest part of bunker play. If you strike the sand a couple of inches or so behind the ball with your sand iron (any other lofted club will work nearly as well), and carry forcefully through with your swing, your ball will be propelled out by the displaced sand. It really is as simple as that.

TOP TO BOTTOM; LEFT TO RIGHT: A normal greenside bunker shot.

ABOVE: Never lash at a bunker shot, as here.

ABOVE: The clubhead has already overtaken the ball because the shot was topped.

Golfers fail to escape from sand for these main reasons:

A *wild 'hit and hope' swing*. Anything can happen, and probably will.

An *indecisive swing*. The player is simply not forceful enough to provide that explosion which blasts that ball up and out.

*Swing* to *the ball, not* through *it*. Perhaps the shot is forceful enough, but the clubhead is merely forced into the sand, rather than through it.

*'Head up'*. The fearful player doesn't really expect to get out. He looks up, at or before the strike, to see the dreaded result. Very likely, that will be a thinned shot which either catches the bunker face, or careers across the green – into more sand, probably.

*Lack of precision*. The basic 'splash' or 'explosion' shot is very simple, but you still have to know where to hit it, and be able to hit where you are aiming. Shots will fail if the clubhead strikes the sand too far away from the ball, or too close to it.

*Playing the shot like a chip*. The player is fearful of taking a full swing and being sufficiently forceful. The fear is that the ball might fly through the green. The tendency is to try to chip the ball out, a rather exact shot at the best of times. This kind of shot could well succeed from firm or wet sand, but failure is likely from a fine, soft surface.

ABOVE: The player's body has straightened up before impact. The result, here, is an air shot.

It's a useful shot to have in your armory when playing an inland course, where, often, there is a clay underlay just beneath the sand. Here, a correctly played sand iron may bounce, and the ball is in danger of flying far beyond the green from a full shot. That kind of disaster can be avoided by playing a chip.

ABOVE: The basic 'splash' shot. Precision is the key.

ABOVE: Clubhead impact with the sand was too far behind the ball. The sand explosion has moved the ball but it has travelled only a small distance and more sideways than forwards.

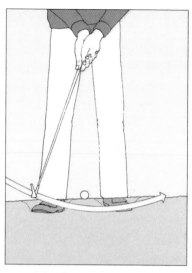

**ABOVE:** Sinking feet into the sand brings club arc below ball.

# GETTING OUT

The first thing to do is to settle your feet firmly down into the sand. This gives you two useful advantages: your feet are firmly anchored, and your club arc is brought lower, roughly where you want it, which is beneath the ball, instead of level with it.

Although the recommendation is to hit the sand about two inches behind the ball, moderate players can minimize the chance of topping the ball by aiming to enter the sand a little further back, say, four to six inches.

The only answer is to practice until you have established a distance that suits you. Let's assume it turns out to be about four inches behind the ball, which will always allow you to take a full backswing and swing freely through the ball. You can then vary that distance by swinging more and less forcefully, and as you gain confidence, you can begin to make your strike closer to the ball.

**ABOVE AND RIGHT:** There was good height on this shot, which reduces run.

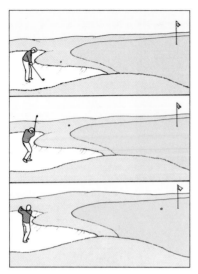

## SHORT SHOTS

Short shots are obviously needed when the flag is close to the greenside bunker – or anyway, quite close. You will inevitably get little backspin, so you can only hope to get your ball close to the hole by correct strength. Height on the ball will create a soft landing, and minimize run.

Stand open, so that you are aiming well to the left of your target. Also, keep the blade of your sand iron well open, but square with a line from ball to hole. The ball should be further forward in your stance than usual, about opposite the left instep.

Try to swing up and down on a fairly steep plane, which will help you gain height. If you take a shallow cut of sand under the ball, both backspin and height will increase, but you'll find that much more precision is needed than when your club enters the sand well behind the ball.

## LONGER SHOTS

Longer shots are necessary when the flag is at the far side of the green, or when the bunker is, say, twenty or thirty yards short of the putting surface.

This time, take a more shallow swing, so that clubhead momentum is less killed because the clubhead is travelling forwards, rather than downwards, and propels sand at the ball more strongly.

This time you'll find that the ball will travel further if you set up square to your target, and keep the clubface square through the ball. Once again, the nearer your strike is to the ball, the more distance you will get.

A long shot from the rear of a bunker.

**TOP, MIDDLE AND ABOVE:** For this longer shot, the blade is squared and the stance less open.

# BACKSPIN

When watching a tournament on TV, you will sometimes be amazed by the amount of backspin a professional gets on a bunker shot. This happens when the player takes the ball directly, without sand intervening between ball and clubface.

However, the pro rarely does this when the flag is near. The shot is reserved for a bunker which is some way short, or wide of, a green. The sand iron is not necessarily the club to use; a wedge, 9-iron and so on may well be preferable.

You can also expect to achieve more backspin from wet sand. Once again, you might try to take the ball directly, avoiding the sand iron because the trailing edge of the flange on the sole of your club may well meet the sand first, and cause the club to bounce. A thinned shot is then the likely result. The relatively sharp leading edges of a wedge or 9-iron will cut into the sand, rather than bounce.

These clubs are also safer to use when your feet tell you that the ground is hard immediately before the top layer of sand, a condition found all too often in badly maintained or constructed bunkers, and usually occurring on inland courses. Once again, by using a wedge or 9-iron you avoid the danger of bounce from the harder clay soil or other material.

This action shot from the bunker clearly shows how much sand is taken.

As the ball is lying on wet sand a 9-iron or wedge are the clubs to use.

Successful bunker play depends upon a good stance and the taking of sand before the ball. Note the divot mark runs parallel to the player's stance because a longer shot has been played.

# BURIED LIES

You will only experience a buried lie when your ball *runs* into a bunker if it does so at speed into soft, fine sand. More often, it arises when your ball has pitched directly into sand, and lies in its pitch mark. On average, about half the ball will lie below the level of the sand, but this very much depends on the firmness of the sand involved. If it's very fine and soft, your ball can disappear altogether.

When playing a bunker shot from a buried lie, you can forget all about the basic sand shot rule of playing with an open blade: impact with the greater body of sand involved is likely to open it even more, providing no real explosion of sand to move the ball on and out.

In fact, there are two quite different ways of playing this type of shot. In the first, you square your blade, play the ball further back in your stance – somewhere about the middle – and then swing far more forcefully than you would for the standard splash shot. You also need to hold your club more firmly than usual, trying to maintain the square face through the impact zone.

Many players fail with this shot simply because they don't swing forcefully enough, worrying perhaps, that they will send the ball many yards through the green. Unless you hit very close to the ball, there's very little danger of that, however.

Unfortunately, you'll get no backspin at all. Your ball will fly low, and because of that, run further than usual. So what's your answer if the flag is quite near the bunker? There isn't

**ABOVE:** The balls lie in their own pitch marks.

one. This is one trouble shot which has no complete answer. Remember – your main aim is to get out of the sand, not get down in two.

Of course, if the hole is at the far side of the green, your troubles decrease. A mixture of good judgement and a little luck may well get you close to your target.

The second method requires you to keep the clubhead square through the stroke by holding the club with the toe turned in, and then swinging as before. The idea is that the turned-in toe makes it much less likely for the clubhead to be forced open through the ball.

Some players use neither of these methods. They use an open face as usual, being confident that they can maintain this position through impact. This is much more dangerous, and may result in your ball travelling a few yards and remaining in the sand. However, there is a better chance of more height on the shot, and therefore less run.

Low flight is, of course, a major problem. Excessive run is one thing, but you have to get out of the bunker first, and how do you do that if your flight isn't high enough?

The answer is quite simple. You don't. You may have to be content to try and escape, and if necessary, accept the penalty of having to play from the sand again if you fail. This time, however, you'll probably have a better lie.

If your bunker isn't particularly deep, but you are confronted by a steep face, take a look around. You may have to abandon all thoughts of playing for the flag and content yourself with escape from the sand, playing out sideways – or even backwards. This will probably mean the loss of a stroke, but that's one hundred per cent better than losing two.

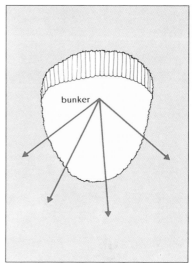

**ABOVE:** Play out sideways or backwards when the face of the bunker is very steep.

**ABOVE:** Squared blade, ball back in stance.

**ABOVE:** Using plenty of clubhead speed.

**ABOVE:** When playing out of a bunker keep your head down.

**ABOVE:** Bunker situations where quick height is needed.

# THE DOWNHILL LIE

This situation arises when your ball has run into sand with very little pace on it, stopping quickly on the slope down to the middle found in most bunkers.

    The danger is that your clubhead will skate over the sand and strike the ball directly, or even thin it. You can reduce this peril by squaring up the blade and playing the ball further back in your stance. From the back of a bunker, you won't often need much height, so you can afford to play with a square club face.

**ABOVE:** Playing from a downhill lie.

# THE UPHILL LIE

Here, your ball will probably have been travelling at speed when it ran into the sand, running on up the face. When playing this shot, you must be wary of striking too far behind the ball, which would entail trying to explode a substantial body of sand at it. This would probably result in a loss of sufficient impetus to move the ball very far.

Obviously enough, the answer is to make your club enter the sand a little closer to the ball, and, as usual, swing firmly through the sand.

**ABOVE:** Playing from an uphill lie.

# DIFFICULT BUNKER STANCES

When your ball is only a short distance into the sand, you may be unable to stand to the ball with both feet in the bunker. This means that your two feet are going to be at significantly different levels.

You probably won't have much difficulty keeping your balance when standing still, but just wait until you try swinging at the ball!

There's no clear solution, and a high-precision shot will probably be impossible, for you or anyone else. However, there's nothing to stop you rehearsing the shot a few times, practicing the swing until you have an indication how forcefully you can swing without losing balance before or at impact. Please feel free to fall over afterwards!

Weigh up the shot and assess your chances of success. If the shot then seems impossible, settle for escape and play out away from the flag.

**ABOVE AND RIGHT:** Playing from an awkward stance.

# UNDER THE FRONT LIP

Quite often, a bunker has an overhanging lip of turf. It's vital to prevent your ball fizzing into this, because it could well plug into the soil, rendering your next shot impossible. It would mean shifting your ball, and a sizeable chunk of turf, onto the green.

Open the club face more than usual, trying for maximum height to get the ball soaring quickly. Swing steeply, both back and down, again hoping to gain maximum height.

**ABOVE:** Plugged in the face. You will have to blast out ball and soil.

# A BARE LIE

Most golfers rake the sand towards them as they retreat after playing their shot. The end result is that, over a period of time, sand becomes more shallow at the centre of the bunker than it is at the edges. Eventually, you get fairly bare lies in the middle, and that condition persists until the bunker is dug out and new sand laid.

Give up any idea of using a sand iron with a high trailing edge, because bounce is likely. Regard the shot as a short pitch, and take the ball clean, using a wedge or 9-iron. If you aren't comfortable with this sort of shot, don't swing too gently.

Any lack of precision in the strike will mean that you won't get the ball out. Play the shot reasonably firmly, accepting that your ball may travel further beyond the hole than you would like.

**ABOVE:** Rake towards the middle of the bunker.

**ABOVE:** This bare lie is the result of the wind.

ABOVE: Fairway bunkers are so placed to 'catch' anything but the best of shots. Fortunately, with the lie of the ball in this bunker there would not be too much difficulty in playing the next shot.

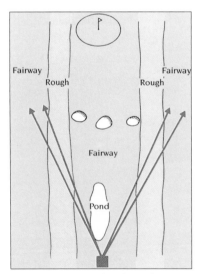

ABOVE: It is not against the rules to play to another fairway to avoid hazards. However, before taking this option make sure the adjacent fairway is clear of players.

# FAIRWAY BUNKERS

When Severiano Ballesteros won his first major Championship, the British Open at Royal Lytham and St Anne's, the number of times he found bunkers caused comment. Royally, Seve declared that it hadn't mattered because "I am the best bunker player".

A few years later, on the Old Course at St Andrews, he became Champion again. It was probably the most consistent performance of his illustrious career, and was, to some extent, based on a strategy of keeping out of bunkers. Indeed, the Spaniard was quite prepared to drive to the fairway of adjacent holes, giving him difficult lines into the greens, just to make sure he did so.

So why such opposing strategies for tackling two different courses?

At Royal Lytham, Seve was mainly catching greenside bunkers and, as we have seen, today's professionals expect to get close to the hole if the ball is lying well in sand. He was confident in getting down in two more. In contrast, at St Andrews he was worried about fairway bunkers, and these can vary dramatically from course to course.

The Old Course has quite deep pot bunkers, from which a player, no matter how skilful, simply can't recover. He is content simply to escape, never mind fly his ball to a green 200 yards away.

There was a contrasting situation in the 1988 US Masters at Augusta National. Sandy Lyle needed to par the final hole to get himself into a sudden-death play-off with Mark Calcavecchia, and took an iron from the tee, aiming to drop short of a fairway bunker on the left.

He struck the ball with just a little draw, went further than he expected, and found the bunker anyway. Was Lyle downcast? Not a bit of it. He saw that his ball was lying cleanly, and not too close to the face, so he could go for the green with a 7-iron. Recovery was entirely possible, even though great precision of strike was needed if he were to whisk the ball! off the surface without taking sand.

As all the world knows, Lyle did better than par. That 7-iron was truly struck, soared over the flag, and the backspin took it back towards the hole. The putt went down, and he was Masters Champion.

Bunkers don't come much tougher than the 'Hell bunker' on the 14th
Fairway at St Andrews which catches the second shot to the green.
This bunker probably cost Gene Sarazen the chance of winning the 1933
British Open.

Another of the many bunkers at St Andrews. This one is a fairway 'pot
bunker' and is difficult to see until close up to. Many unsuspecting
golfers fall foul of such bunkers.

ABOVE: No chance of making great distance from a deep fairway bunker.

# DEEP FAIRWAY BUNKERS

These reduce all good golfers to around the same level. No one can recover from them and hit a distant green.

All you can do is concentrate on getting out, and being sure of landing in a good position for your next shot. There's no point at all in knocking your ball into another trap. It also makes sense to aim for a target of some sort, just as you would from a greenside bunker. This could be a flat area of fairway, or a position which gives you a good approach to the flag. You could also consider a spot which will enable you to hit a favorite club with plenty of backspin.

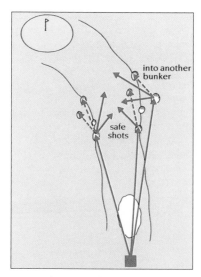

ABOVE: Make sure you don't escape from one bunker into another.

# RECOVERY SHOTS

You've made a mistake and hit sand. To 'recover', in this context, means to play a sand shot which leaves you in a position as good as you would have been in if you hadn't found the bunker in the first place. This is usually possible only if your ball is lying clean, and not too close to the front face or any of the lips.

If there's no face at all, but just the front lip of a very shallow bunker, then your problems are less severe: you don't have to calculate how much loft your club should have to make sure of getting out. If there is a face, you need to visualize the trajectories you will get from various clubs. Having done that – take one more for safety, because if you fail to escape you'll be in a worse position than ever, close up to the face, or even plugged into it.

Settle your feet firmly into the sand, and shorten your grip on the club. This helps compensate for the fact that your feet are below the level of the ball, and the shortened shaft gives you a more precise strike. Don't overswing going back, because your stance is less secure on sand than it would be on turf. Swing normally, concentrating, even more than usual, on finding the back of the ball with the middle of the clubhead.

This avoids two potential disasters when playing sand shots: catching the sand just behind the ball, and thinning the shot. The first produces a very weak result, losing a great deal of distance, and perhaps even keeping you in the bunker. The second is usually caused by sheer anxiety, making you look up before you hit.

Your choice of club is wide open. Given a good strike, a 3-wood can be played successfully, and so can a long iron, but don't forget that longer shafts are more demanding on your precision.

The answer lies in experiment and practice. You may learn that you can't really trust yourself with anything more demanding than a 5-iron, let's say. So you accept the limitation, and you'll find you can still go for the green quite often, and if you're bunkered on the tee from a par 5, you'll still gain useful distance.

There is a tendency to get one club less distance from sand, and also to fade the ball. Just make allowances.

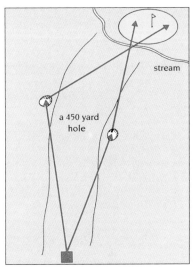

**ABOVE:** These are true recovery shots. The player is on the green in two.

**ABOVE:** The ball is sitting up on the sand, well away from the front lip. A long recovery shot should be possible.

**ABOVE:** From this good lie, a 3-wood could be played but this front lip might catch the ball.

# RULES AND BEHAVIOR IN SAND

I happen to believe that bunkers should punish a poor shot.
That's what they're there for. Pine Valley, is an example of an
attitude which I admire – that a bunker should sometimes be
an unraked wilderness, and expanse designed to fill a golfer
with apprehension.

Oakmont also used to be an example of terror bunkers –
but they don't do it right any more. Until recent years they
had a device which raked bunkers into a series of furrows,
rather than into a level surface. There was hardly a ball which
didn't nestle down into a trough. All you could expect of an
Oakmont bunker was what today's golfers would call a 'bad
lie'. You could get your ball out, but full recovery shots were
seldom possible.

"Fine," say I. Every golfer expects to lose a shot when in
the water, so why should sand be any different?

I accept that I'm in a minority, and I don't carry on a one-
man protest movement by refusing to rake the sand over
when I've played my shot – but many golfers do, especially if
they haven't recovered well. Why should the next fellow not
suffer too?

**ABOVE:** A grass island in a bunker isn't part of
the hazard.

**ABOVE:** The club has been grounded.

**ABOVE:** As this is a practice bunker it is less frequently raked, so you have more chance to practice your recovery shots.

**ABOVE:** According to the rules of golf, man-made objects may be moved, if they impede your shot.

**ABOVE:** Look at the local rules before removing stones.

After you've played your shot, do use the rake usually provided to efface your sand divot and your footmarks. If you are really concerned about maintaining, and even improving, course conditions, don't be content with raking the sand out from the middle out to the edges as you retreat. That's what the rest of the world does, and it leads to the condition discussed under 'Bare Lies', where the sand becomes more shallow towards the centre than at the edges. Push sand towards the middle, rather than dragging it to the edge.

Sometimes, you won't be able to find a rake, but don't just shrug your shoulders and walk on. Smooth the surface with your feet as you retreat – much more effective than using your sand iron.

If there is a rake, you must remember to replace it. Sometimes there's no problem because a rake holder is provided. If not, note the custom at the course you're playing. Some seem to prefer rakes to be parked close by the bunker, others in the sand itself.

The second alternative would seem more logical: a rake left in the sand can neither divert a ball into the bunker, or prevent it from going in.

Remember the rules about grounding your club. You aren't allowed to ground your club in any hazard, and a bunker is certainly one of these. However, the grassy banks surrounding most bunkers aren't part of the hazard, and neither is any timber shoring, so you don't incur a penalty if you touch them, something all too easy to do during your backswing. A grass island in the bunker itself doesn't count as a hazard, either.

You are always allowed to move any loose impediments interfering with your shot, anywhere on a golf course – except in a hazard. So don't bend down and pick up any leaf, twig or stone which you'd like out of the way. There can be exceptions, however. Tournament professionals, for example, are allowed to pamper themselves more than we ordinary mortals, and may usually pick up stones. Even they can **sometimes find themselves penalized for doing so when** playing in an event such as an Open Championship not covered by the slightly modified rules used on the US and European Tours.

Your scorecard can sometimes give you a pleasant surprise. If a stone is interfering with your shot, you will sometimes find a local rule allowing you to lift it.

There is also relief without penalty from scrapes and holes in sand made by burrowing animals. You are allowed a free drop, just so long as you stay in the bunker. The same is true of casual water.

Again, sometimes a bunker may be undergoing repair, and is marked as 'GUR'. In this case you are allowed to drop without penalty. In all these cases of relief, you are not allowed, of course, to drop nearer the hole.

You are not allowed to clear sand away from your ball in order to identify it, even if you find it half buried. This isn't quite so severe as it sounds, because there is no penalty for playing the wrong ball, in this case. Have a look at it once you are out of the sand, and if it turns out to be the wrong one, retrace your steps and play again.

But what if you can't even find the ball, yet you are absolutely certain you saw it plummet down into the sand? Here you have two alternatives. You can institute a search with no penalty for touching the sand, but once a ball has been detected, it must be played without removing all the sand you might like in order to make sure it's yours. If, in spite of all the searching, the ball cannot be found, even though you 'know' the ball is in the bunker, you just have to declare it lost and retrace your steps to play your shot again under stroke and distance penalty.

It's a hard world, but at least this is only likely to occur in the finest of coastal sand.

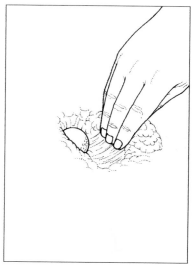

**ABOVE:** Once you see the ball, you aren't allowed to remove sand to identify it.

# IN THE ROUGH

There are two distinct types of rough. The grass can be *long*, or it can be *dense*.

Grass which is long need not be a problem if it's thin and wispy. It may tend to wrap around your blade, but this won't usually prevent you playing an effective shot. Contrast that with the experiences at the 1990 US PGA Championship, where the rough was deep in a different sense, and balls became buried in it when only just off the greens and fairways. If it hadn't been for the presence of marshals and spectators, many more balls would have been lost, even though they resulted from shots which were by no means poor ones.

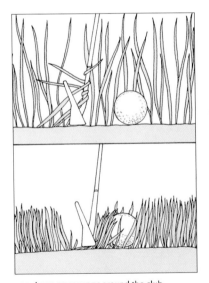

**TOP:** Long grass wraps around the club.

**ABOVE:** The ball is buried although the grass is only about 2 inches long.

**ABOVE:** Spectators and marshals find many errant balls.

# IN DEEP ROUGH

It is reported that the editor of a well-known magazine dropped his watch while adjusting it, and took a long time to find it – just off the green.

From this kind of rough it's often impossible to play a recovery shot. Even steely-wristed professionals find they need too much strength to cut through the grass, and then *force* the ball through for any substantial distance. The only remedy is to accept the loss of a shot, select a highly lofted club in order to gain height quickly and move the ball back into play – perhaps only 50 or 100 yards onwards.

When your ball is a long way off line, and therefore far from the fairway, you may have to accept no gain in distance at all, and play out sideways.

Club choice has to vary, according to the severity of the lie. In the worst situations, the sand iron, with its extra weight and maximum loft, is the club to use. In fact, you need loft

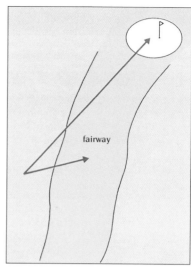

**ABOVE:** When the ball is in very dense or long grass, play back to the fairway instead of to the green.

**ABOVE:** You can get out of this but not make a full recovery.

**ABOVE AND RIGHT:** Getting out with a sand iron.

**ABOVE AND RIGHT:** Sometimes you have to play back to the fairway (the green is extreme right).

more than anything else in order to get the ball out of the clinging grass quickly, so you should never use a straight-faced club once your ball is in an unfavorable lie.

You will also tend to close the face of the club as you force through to the ball, and longer irons then become totally ineffective. Arnold Palmer found this out when playing in the 1966 US Open at Olympic.

In the final round, he was heading for a new Championship scoring record. Only Billy Casper was in any sort of contact, and he was several shots behind.

Then Palmer tried a long iron from dense rough, and his ball died in as bad a position, not many yards further on. In the end, Caspar overhauled him, and Palmer never won another major Championship. He probably still thinks how different things might have been if he'd used a wedge, rather than an iron, that day.

The tendency for the face to close in the impact zone can be counteracted if you set up the clubface more open than usual before gripping. You will also need to grip more firmly than usual, and maintain that firmness through the ball. Strength isn't usually as important as clubhead speed in the game of golf, but this is one occasion when sheer brawn is useful.

# BURIED LIES IN ROUGH

You also need strength to maintain the grip and fast hands to get you out of buried lies in the grass. Many players, in this situation, are far too optimistic. They visualize the perfect result, and forget that they can't always achieve this, even from good lies, so do be realistic in assessing your chances. It pays to make sure of moving your ball out to a position where you can resume playing the hole.

Sometimes, even this isn't possible, as Ben Hogan found when playing the 1955 US Open, again at Olympic.

He was playing off with the unknown, Jack Fleck, over 18 holes, and was trying for a record fifth Open Championship as well. At the last, he played a quick hook from the tee, and landed in very dense rough. Using a lofted club, and aiming only to get back to the fairway, he needed three attempts, being able to move his ball only for short distances each time. Once there, he got down with an iron to the green and one putt – which shows how important it is to get into a position where you can continue to play the hole.

Hogan was one stroke behind Fleck playing this short par 4 hole, so couldn't afford an option he might have taken earlier in the play-off. (Fleck was well down the fairway, and there was no reason why he shouldn't make his par 4.)

He could have declared his ball unplayable, and then walked back, as far as he liked, until he found more favorable ground to drop his ball. I remember watching Tom Weiskopf doing this at the only major Championship he ever won, the 1973 British Open at Troon. He hit one drive which finished well down in the gorse, a position which gave him a fair chance of getting his ball back to the fairway – but a fair chance of failure, too. Tom decided that the risks weren't acceptable, and he picked up his ball under penalty and walked back, perhaps 100 yards, until he came upon a good lie.

Although a 6 went on his card, it could have been much worse, and a day later he was Champion. You couldn't say that that decision won him his Championship, but the wrong one could certainly have lost it for him.

**OPPOSITE:** These shots pose many problems. Getting the clubhead through all that grass is the biggest problem which is why it is best to select the heaviest club in your bag – a wedge or 9-iron. You won't get much distance but you should, hopefully, get out of trouble.

**ABOVE AND RIGHT:** When the ball is well down, use a lofted club.

## SEMI-ROUGH

In US and European Tour events, as well as top amateur matches, rules are laid down concerning the length to which semi-rough should be cut. But, as I have just stressed, density of grass is far more important. Lies found in semi-rough can vary enormously.

Your ball can be sitting up as if on a tee peg, and from such a lie you can use a driver more easily than a good fairway lie. On the other hand, it may be nestling down at the roots, and a wedge back into play may well be the most sensible club selection.

You will, however, encounter conditions as extreme as this very seldom, perhaps only when grass growth is at its peak. So ignore the term 'semi-rough' and think solely about how your ball is situated. As I've said, a driver could be appropriate, if you need distance, and you can always consider taking a wood, even though you might eventually decide against it.

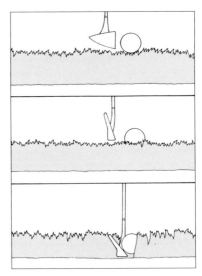

**TOP:** If the ball is perched on the grass, you can play another wood.

**ABOVE CENTER:** The ball is only a little down in the grass so a long iron is possible.

**BOTTOM:** When the ball is in long grass you need a sand iron.

In the semi-rough a wood may be used if the ball is sitting up well on the grass.

A 7 being used from a reasonable lie.

When you need a long shot, there are some easy decisions to be made. A wooden clubhead pushes its way through grass, while an iron cuts through. Once you decide a wood isn't safe, you certainly shouldn't be thinking of – for example – a 3– or 4–iron. Your decision and your choice of club should be far more drastic. Think in terms of no less a degree of loft than 6.

Another useful club to have in your bag is a wood with a small head; a number 5, perhaps, or even the less-often seen number 7. These small-headed clubs are splendid for getting through grass, even moderately dense. They also make a useful substitute for players who aren't really happy with long irons at any time.

It is possible to use long irons from the semi-rough, depending on the lie. However, for most people they should be avoided at all costs, unless the lie of the ball offers no problems at all.

ABOVE: A wood pushes through the grass.

ABOVE: An iron has to cut through the grass.

ABOVE: The size of wooden clubheads can vary enormously.

**ABOVE:** Playing an iron from a good lie in the semi-rough.

# BAD LIES IN THE ROUGH

As I've said earlier, you have to be prepared to sacrifice
distance towards the green, and settle for playing out
sideways. Sometimes, even this isn't an option and you take a
penalty drop in kinder country. If you find you have a bad lie,
but still think you can move your ball back to the fairway, how
do you play the shot?

The answer is something like that for a bunker shot.
Open the face before gripping, to compensate for the
tendency for the face to close around impact, and play with a
steeper swing arc, breaking the wrists early. Almost
automatically, you will then swing back to the ball more
steeply, and your ball should rise quickly, helping you to get
up and clear of the grass.

An open face is essential if you want the ball to
clear the grass.

# THE FLYER

The normal way to play an iron shot squeezes the ball between clubhead and turf. This promotes backspin, but also reduces the speed of the ball. When your ball is resting on grass, and therefore is raised off the ground, this squeezing effect can't happen. You are whisking it off the grass, and the result is a considerably longer shot: backspin is reduced, and there is no friction between clubhead, ball and turf.

Only experience can teach you just how much further your ball will travel, and no one can ever be totally sure.

Seve Ballesteros had to use this kind of judgement and experience when playing the 17th, or Road Hole, at the Old Course at St Andrews, arguably golf's most difficult par hole.

It happened at the climax of the 1984 British Open, when Seve and Tom Watson were level. The Spaniard drove down into the left rough, when the only way to make a second shot along the line of the green possible is to drive close to out-of-bounds on the right.

But Seve had to come in from the side, and had only a few yards to play with, because a little short would have landed him in the Road bunker. Getting down in two from there is unlikely, because the flag is always set close to it in Championships. A touch too strong, and his ball would have run on into the road along the right of the green.

He examined his lie, and decided it was a flying one. Instead of selecting, say, a 4–iron, he took a 6. The shot was exact for distance, and had enough backspin to hold the green. About a quarter of a hour later he was Champion.

It had been a superb shot – but luck also smiled on him.

That's one kind of flyer. The second is quite different. When your ball is in semi-rough, or perhaps in longer grass, it can often lie with only the top half exposed. When your club meets the ball, there will be a cushion of grass in between. You can easily see just how much, when you examine the lie.

This cushion has two effects. When there are just a few blades between clubface and ball it will make little difference to the speed at which ball leaves clubhead – but backspin is considerably reduced.

Because backspin causes the ball to climb, you will have only the loft given by the angle of the clubface to rely on. Reduced backspin when the ball comes to earth will mean far less bite, and your ball will therefore run further.

Only experience of playing similar shots over months and years with the same club will tell you just how much further.

Playing from rough of any kind usually leaves grass remains compacted into the grooves on your club. Wet grass can clean them out, or in dry conditions, a little scraping with a tee peg will partly do the job.

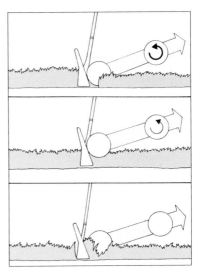

**TOP:** The club squeezes the ball against the turf, causing good backspin.

**ABOVE CENTER:** The ball is resting on the grass, so there is little backspin.

**BOTTOM:** There is no backspin when grass comes between the ball and the clubface.

**ABOVE:** The grooves of the iron can be cleaned with a tee peg.

317

LEFT: The Road bunker at St Andrews. Seve had to fly it but not run across the narrow green into the road beyond. (In championship play, the flag is always set near the Road bunker. Here it is towards the front of the green.)

When lobbing from deep grass allow for side spin.

**BELOW AND OPPOSITE:** Playing the lob. Notice the open stance and that the clubhead is cutting across the ball parallel to the feet.

# DEEP OR THICK ROUGH BY THE GREENSIDE

So far, we have been considering playing techniques and options when the aim is either to escape, or to play to a green some considerable distance away. If, however, you're in this kind of trouble just a few yards from the putting surface, you aren't usually going to be satisfied with merely hacking it out. You'll want to be on the green, preferably close to the hole and so you must consider the options available.

The main problem is that grass intervening between ball and clubhead will deprive you of backspin. So in this case it is recommended that you substitute height, with the result that your ball plummets *downwards* rather than *forwards* when it pitches.

To achieve this, you play the lob, which is rather like a bunker splash shot. Open the stance, stand with the ball opposite your left instep, and set the clubface open, aiming at the flag, or even a little to the left, to take into account the left-to-right sidespin you should get. Take a bunker-length backswing – about three-quarters – and swing freely through the hitting area.

Things become even more like a bunker shot when you don't think you can get your clubhead to the ball directly. Aim to make contact a few inches behind the ball, and add a little more swing pace, enabling your club to slide through the resistance offered by the grass.

This is not as difficult to play as the cut-up shot from a good fairway lie, because that needs great strike precision. Because you should get the ball up and out quickly, you won't be left woefully contemplating a ball which has moved just a foot or two, smothered by grass.

You don't always have to play the lob from long greenside grass. If you have a clear path into your ball, and a reasonable lie, play a normal short pitch with a lofted club.

**ABOVE AND RIGHT:** Playing the lob from a better lie. The open stance and follow through remain the same.

# LOOSE LIES

Golf balls often come to rest on loose divots, leaves, pine needles, small twigs and other moveable objects. The operative word here is 'moveable'. Outside of bunkers, you can pick up and toss away anything which impedes your stroke or – particularly when putting or chipping – which your ball may strike later on. When this material is not too close to the ball, there's no real problem, although you do have to be careful that the material is dead and not growing material still attached to the ground. You are not allowed, under the rules of the game, to pull up wispy grass by the roots.

Because someone hasn't replaced a divot this player is now faced with an awkward shot which requires a lofted club. To make sure you are never faced with this shot, replace divots. This way eventually this sort of shot will be eliminated.

You can't avoid falling leaves and if your ball lands on one it is unfortunate. Because the removal of the leaf would cause your ball to move you have to play the shot as it lies.

This stone is a 'moveable' object under the rules but you must make sure your ball does not move in the process of removing it.

Moving the leaf would cause the ball to move which is not allowed.

Moving this twig would cause the ball to move which is not allowed.

Because the tree is marked, a drop without penalty is permitted.

Your judgement has to come into play once such objects are closer to the ball. Even if you are still some distance away and tread on one end of a twig, which then moves and in turn moves the ball – that's a penalty. So tread carefully.

Once you get to the ball, examine material which might affect your shot. Most important is anything you will strike before impact with the ball. Even a small twig, intervening between clubface and ball at impact can cause a disaster. Get rid of such things – but first make sure your ball doesn't move as a result.

The dangers of inadvertently moving your ball are still not quite over. You have yet to take your stance and address the ball. Causing the ball to move when grounding your club close to it is always a possibility. So, if there's a danger here – don't ground your club. This isn't a new situation, because you already avoid grounding when in a bunker or in water.

Some golfers never ground clubs, believing that this prevents touching the turf at the beginning of a backswing, and avoids a tendency to lift the club at the start.

Those fallen leaves (and twig) again! This time they are easily removed but take care when doing so.

When playing from this lie you have to make contact with the leaf before the ball.

Having taken all these precautions – which takes much longer to write about than actually to do when out on the course – you must then make small adjustments to the way you play the shot. Precision is the main thing: you need to whisk the ball off the loose surface, rather than hitting down on to that cushion of leaves or pine needles. This isn't a situation for a full-out shot: grip a little lower down and swing easily, concentrating on an exact strike, rather than on clubhead speed.

You can usually ignore objects which your ball will contact immediately after impact. A ball brushing a leaf aside won't be much affected. It's rather different, however, when the leaves come before the ball, because they will cushion the shot and deprive you of some backspin. Make allowances. These situations won't happen all that often in a golfing lifetime, so you won't have experience to draw upon. Rely on your imagination to tell you how the ball will behave.

If anything is still growing then you cannot remove it. The simple rule is: If it's dead then it can be removed, provided it doesn't cause your ball to move.

# RULES AND BEHAVIOR IN THE ROUGH

Rough, though it may be punishing, isn't classed as a hazard under the rules of golf, so there are no special rules to worry about.

This means that you are allowed to identify your ball positively, and are penalized if you fail to do so and play the wrong ball. You are permitted to move the grass in order to do so, but must not improve your lie.

Be careful how you address your ball. Causing it to move costs one penalty stroke, so it's wise to avoid grounding your club if there's any chance of this happening. But what does 'moving the ball' mean?

It means making the ball move from its original position, and coming to rest in another one. This may be just a fraction of an inch, but if your ball merely rocks and settles back into its original position, then that does not constitute movement in golf, and there's no penalty.

If your ball is so deeply entangled that you judge there is no chance of moving it, even with a sand iron, you can, any time, anywhere on the course, declare it unplayable. This leaves you with three options. The first is to take your penalty drop within two club lengths, and no nearer the hole.

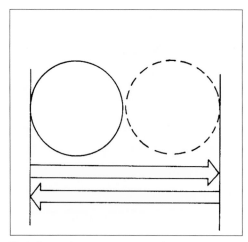

The ball moves but returns to its original position, therefore there is no penalty.

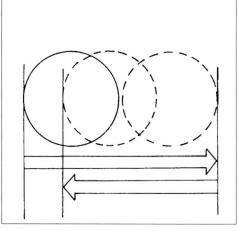

When the ball oscillates but comes to a lie a fraction of an inch away from its original position, you have to take the penalty.

**ABOVE:** You can choose a drop if you decide a shot is unplayable.

However, as you survey the local scene, you could well decide that such a drop would leave you in an equally unpromising situation. You might finish in just as difficult a lie – but without the option of trying again, except with the loss of another penalty shot. If so, you can walk back to the tee, or to any other place from which you struck the ball, and play your shot again, under penalty.

However, you can save distance by taking the third option. Walk back, keeping your lie between you and the hole, until you find a suitable place to drop.

# IN WATER

When your ball finishes in water, you normally have no problem at all. It's a lost ball, or an irretrievable one, and you just have to accept your one stroke penalty and play on with no pause for thought.

At other times, it will be in clear sight, and decision time. Do you play a shot or retrieve your ball? There is at least one case on record where the decision to play was taken rather to extremes.

In around 1912, a player in the qualifying round of the Shawnee Invitational for Ladies at Shawnee-on-Delaware, Pennsylvania, sent her tee shot, at the short 16th, into the Binniekill River – and it floated. Her husband, rather sadistically you might say, bundled her into a boat and took the oars.

**ABOVE:** If it's in the middle, accept your penalty shot.

**TOP AND ABOVE:** Drop another and play on.

When playing a short shot over water play
it like a lob, making sure the stance is
open.

She eventually got the boat ashore after a multitude of attemps a mile-and-a-half downstream, and then had to play through a wood on her way back to the fairway. She eventually sank her putt, having taken 166 strokes. Not bad for a 130-yard hole!

I'm not suggesting you go to those extremes. Indeed, one decision you must make when your ball is in water is whether you are willing to risk injury or not. Water is hard stuff when you swing a golf club into it at speed, and hand or wrist injury is quite likely if you attempt to play a forceful shot through it.

There's probably no point in taking the risk, however. The water will slow your clubhead speed by a considerable amount, and there will also be a similar effect on the ball. Even if your clubhead does have significant momentum left when it meets the ball, escape proves impossible because of the water's resistance to the ball itself.

The rule of thumb must be – don't attempt to play out of water if the whole of the ball is below the surface. The chances of injury are substantial, and of success negligible. Take your penalty drop: it's only one stoke.

You may remember Payne Stewart playing the last hole at The Belfry, at the end of his Ryder Cup singles match in 1989. His unsuccessful attempts to move his ball from the front edge of a lake to the fairway would never have been made in stroke play. In his particular matchplay situation, he had little to lose. If he had taken his penalty stroke, he would still have lost the hole, and the match, to Jose-Maria Olazabal.

It is safest to make it your rule not to attempt to play a water shot unless at least half of your ball is exposed. But it also depends where your ball actually is.

The best advice is to pick and drop and forfeit one stroke. It could cost you more if you attempt these shots with a submerged ball.

The temptation may be to try and play this ball out but don't forget you got in the mess in the first place. So, realistically assess your chances of improving the situation from there.

You may have a playable lie from water but even the best players can make a hash of such shots.

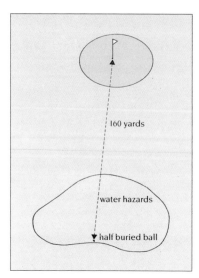

160 yards

water hazards

▼ half buried ball

**ABOVE:** If you cannot reach the green it is sensible to drop out of the hazard for a 1 stroke penalty.

# IN A STREAM

Here, you will usually be faced by a bank, so you need to get your ball up quickly. In this case, think along the same lines as you would if you were in a bunker. If you have strong doubts whether you can achieve enough height quickly enough to escape, don't try it. Accept your penalty stroke.

Your ball will usually be set upon a firm surface, sometimes small pebbles or gravel, and they could help, although they might chip your clubhead.

You'll be unfamiliar with playing from water, so it's essential to maintain confidence. Make up your mind how you're going to play your shot, and stick to your decision.

The club to use is often a sand iron, especially if you're actually swinging through water. It's the heaviest in your set, and has the most loft to help you get height quickly.

It's also worth weighing up the distance you are going to achieve. If you believe you can reach the green, for example, then go ahead. If, however, you are merely playing out, expecting to gain 20 yards or so, then there's little point in taking the risk. You'll be just as well off if you drop out under penalty, and hopefully, in a lie which will allow you to use a full 3-wood if you need maximum distance.

**ABOVE AND RIGHT:** The ball has to rise quickly.

**LEFT, BELOW AND BELOW LEFT:**
Playing from a soft, wet lie –
but the ball isn't under water.

**ABOVE:** The ball is on a firm surface.

**RIGHT:** From a bad lie, could you be sure to clear this expanse of water? If not, take your penalty drop.

# IN POND OR LAKE

In this situation, you may well be lying on soft mud, and in that case, you have to feel sure that you can get your clubhead under the ball. Hitting an inch or so behind the ball, as in a bunker shot, isn't likely to work, because your clubhead will simply bury itself in the ooze, and transfer little forward momentum to the ball.

From an expanse of water, you are unlikely to need a quickly rising shot – unless you have only just failed to carry the water and are on the far side. However, you will often find you need considerable length. If so, don't try it, because the chances of success are slight.

This ball is playable but, in view of the muddy conditions, make sure you have a towel handy ready to clean your face and clubs!

# RULES AND CONDUCT WHEN IN WATER

The first thing to remember is that at no time must your club touch the water, at address or backswing. If it does, you lose one penalty stroke. The same applies anywhere in a water hazard, so be wary once you are inside the marked area, on a bank, for example.

You must also remember that a water hazard – lake, pond, stream, river or ditch – doesn't have to contain any water. The water hazard is the area marked as such. In theory, this could be any area; even a rough circle marked on a flat fairway could count as a water hazard.

Don't ground your club in a water hazard.

The red marker indicates this is a lateral water hazard and the rules governing it are different to those for a normal water hazard.

In real life, however, streams and the like can dry up in drought, just as lakes and ponds can, and the extent to which this happens often varies widely during a golfing year. Whatever the case, you are still in the water area if you are within the form of marking used – usually stakes.

But don't be too carelessly overjoyed if you find your ball in a water hazard but on dry land. Hazard rules still apply, and you will be penalized if you ground your club. If the ball is nestling in deep vegetation, you are not allowed to identify it, but as in sand, you are not penalized if you play the wrong ball, but immediately replay the shot.

The rules for natural loose impediments are just the same as those for sand. You may not move them. If, for example, a large branch prevents you playing your shot, you simply drop out of the hazard, under penalty.

A lateral water hazard doesn't only have to be in the form of a stream or river running alongside the fairway, it can be in the form of a pond.

A ditch, whether it contains water or not, is still defined as a water hazard.

ABOVE: Boarded banks define a water hazard clearly.

No water in sight, but this is still termed a water
hazard under the rules.

Casual water is any temporary accumulation on the course and is NOT a water hazard.

## CASUAL WATER

Casual water is all water not normally a part of the course, and is usually the result of heavy rain, or even of an incursion by the sea. Being casual, it will not be marked as a hazard. You can lift and drop your ball without penalty from these unusual ground conditions.

You are also entitled to relief when you, rather than the ball, are in the water, when taking up your stance. The water doesn't have to be covering the surface. You can claim relief if water appears when your body weight causes it to rise and become visible around your shoes.

# OTHER HAZARDS

As the term suggests, bare lies occur when your ball is resting on the surface, without a covering of grass. It generally occurs on courses where there is more traffic than usual, or on small high spots where the grass dies off in dry weather.

Full shots ought to cause relatively little trouble, although of course, the ball is not 'sitting up' as so many golfers prefer for fairway wood shots. Many good players, however, prefer to use an iron from bare lies, or 'hard pan' as such lies are usually known in America and Australia. This is because there just isn't any grass between clubface and ball, making distance and the amount of backspin occurring, much more easy to predict.

For full shots with any club, from driver to sand iron, the best method is to make sure that you striking *down* on the ball. That's because there is less margin for error than if you attempt to sweep it away, as you might with a driver, for example. After all, the ball isn't sitting on a tee peg of grass.

To help you hit slightly downwards, move the ball back

in your stance, an inch or two further than you usually would for that particular club, and swing freely. Grip the club a little further down the shaft to help you achieve a more precise strike.

Shorter clubs are rather more difficult. When close to a green with an obstacle to clear – and even if there isn't one – most professionals reach for their sand iron, wanting maximum height and backspin. Unfortunately, you may find, when you address the ball, that the absence of that cushion of grass makes the trailing edge of the sand iron meet the ground before the leading edge does. At best, that means that it is difficult to get the leading edge under the ball. You may not think it, but however precise your stroke, you will meet the ball a little above the lowest point. The shot might just come off perfectly, but it isn't any too likely.

**ABOVE:** A sand iron is not appropriate on hard ground. The trailing edge of the iron would meet the ground first.

**ABOVE:** Strike down on the ball when it comes to rest on a bare lie, in this case re-seeded divots.

At worst, the trailing edge may meet the ground first, the club bounces, and the ball scuttles away on a low trajectory, right through the green.

However, there's an obvious answer to this problem. Set up for the shot with the ball further back in your stance, hands well ahead, until you find that the leading edge will meet the ground first.

Unfortunately, this delofts your sand iron. Unless you very much prefer using this club for this kind of shot, you may just as well modify your club selection and opt for a pitching wedge.

Whichever club you use, however, avoid a short backswing, which will almost certainly make you jab at the ball. The swing should be at least to shoulder height, and you should then gently accelerate the clubhead, making sure you don't slow down before impact.

Set your weight a little more on the front foot, and swing back steeply. Give yourself the feeling, as you come into the ball, that you are dropping the clubhead down to it.

A high spot.

**TOP, ABOVE LEFT AND CENTER:** Chipping from a bare lie. The player was anxious and lifted his head too soon. The ball finished in the bunker to his right.

**RIGHT:** Here the shot is better and avoids the bunker.

## DIVOT MARKS

On some holes, a high proportion of tee shots seem to come to rest in the same area – at the foot of a slope, or in a hollow, for example. The fairway will be heavily scarred by divots, in that area, and therefore, your chances of coming to rest in one are high.

One problem about this is that the head of your golf club may not fit into the divot mark, especially if you are thinking of playing a long iron. In that case, the rounded sole of a fairway wood might be a better option. If you don't need maximum distance, grip down the shaft and don't hit full out.

**RIGHT:** On extremely used patches of fairway, the ball is likely to come to rest in a divot.

**LEFT:** A long iron overlaps the divot mark.

You are likely to take some turf before you make contact, so play the ball back in your stance, with more weight on your front foot, than for a normal shot, and swing in steeply. Don't just punch your clubhead into the ground – keep it flowing through impact.

With the ball back in your stance, you can expect low flight, and consequently more run on the ball. This might not be a problem, unless you need to clear an obstacle such as a greenside bunker, and then want the ball to stop quickly.

If this is the case, you have a decision to make. If you are a good bunker player, you might even play for it, or accept the fact that your punch shot will finish far past the flag.

The alternative is to concentrate on exact striking, and play for a more normal shot, with the ball inside left heel, but play with a slightly open blade, break the wrists sharply on the backswing – creating a steep swing path – and swing back with a steeper path than usual.

Playing from a divot isn't usually particularly difficult, just so long as you take care. However, if the divot is deep, it may become impossible to achieve an ideal result. If so, accept it, and be content to do no more than play for a good position for your next shot.

**ABOVE AND RIGHT:** Playing out of a divot. Set the ball back in your stance and make sure you swing through. We have already told you how to avoid this shot but it is worth reiterating: replace all divots which you have made.

**ABOVE AND RIGHT:** Your ball may come to rest to the front or rear of a divot.

This is an unfortunate lie but you ought to get relief for unusual ground conditions. If not you could only hope to explode it out.

# EXTREME STANCES

Having learned how to play all the shots with a normal stance on a flat lie, you rapidly discover that there are many occasions in a golfing year when you have to play from very uncomfortable positions. By 'uncomfortable' I don't mean stances which involve you in actual physical pain, such as having to back into a bush with cactus-like prickles, but those which arise when it's impossible to stand to the ball at all normally.

This normally involves standing with one foot on a vastly different level from the other.

There are various occasions when this might happen. Sometimes, an opponent, seeing the result of a less-than-perfect shot will comment how lucky you were not to have found sand – but this isn't always the case Often, being just not quite in the sand will put you in a more difficult situation that actually finding yourself in it. Playing with one foot in a bunker and the other out, is never easy, and the deeper the bunker, the more difficult it is.

Much the same situation arises when you aren't quite in a water hazard. With luck, you won't have to get your feet wet, because you can find a foot placement on the bank, but you still have that very uneven stance.

Balls that miss greens leaving you short, or to either side, often finish on banks, most times leaving you with an uphill shot. Those that run through the putting surface may well find a bank at the back, presenting you with a downhill shot.

Although these situations *seem* very different, in the end, they give rise to the same range of extreme stances. The ball can be either well above or well below your feet, or your two feet can be at very different levels.

**ABOVE:** Both feet in a bunker isn't an easy situation. Grip right down the shaft.

**RIGHT AND OPPOSITE:** You must limit your ambition playing with feet at different levels.

## UP A STEEP BANK

Here, it won't often be very difficult to balance, and the fact that the back of the ball will usually be exposed is also helpful: you might even be able to see the very bottom of it. As steep banks usually occur near greens, it's unlikely that you will have to use much power. But there are occasions which disprove this rule. You might, for example, hit a wild tee shot and finish up among dunes on a link course, or some artful architect may even have contrived some humps for you.

Because of the slope, most of your weight will be thrown on the back foot. You can live with that, providing you only need a fairly gentle swing. Set up with the ball towards your front foot, and don't forget that you'll need to judge the loft of the club needed. Anything at all straight faced is likely to knock your ball straight into the turf, because of the severe slope in front of the ball. Keep your body out of the shot, and **visualize yourself playing almost entirely with hands-and-**arms action. Rehearse the shot to see how to maintain balance.

**ABOVE:** Not too difficult to maintain balance even on this steep slope – as long as you don't need a full swing.

Often, the sand iron will be the club to use because you will get quick height from it, and that steep slope behind the ball means that there is no danger of the sole flange catching the ball and bouncing.

When attempting longer shots, however, you won't want to use the sand iron, because you'll get so little length from it. How far you can move the ball depends on your ability to maintain your balance as you increase swing speed.

A practice swing or two will tell you how far you can go – and if you fall over, then you'd better decrease both your swing speed and your ambitions.

These ought to be fairly limited, anyway, and on very severe slopes, you can't expect to wind up your body and still retain balance. Stick to hands-and-arms action, with not too much shoulder and hip turn. Also remember to allow for the fact that you'll get more height than usual with the club you select.

**ABOVE:** Dunes on a links course.

## DOWN A STEEP BANK

This is a far more difficult proposition. Take the tricky matter of balance.

Any reasonably vigorous shot will force you to transfer your weight wholly to the front foot, which may already be finding it difficult to find a firm foothold on that steep slope. You are certain to topple forwards – not that that's any real problem, just so long as you've got the ball away first.

Getting at the back of the ball on a steep downslope can be a very severe problem. The situation is exactly the converse to the one faced on upslopes, because the geometry is against you. That downslope actually shields the back of the ball.

First, set up the ball well back in your stace. Depending on the severity of the slope, this can be very far back indeed – even behind your right foot. This helps you come down sharply on the ball, and to get into the back of it. You will also need to pick the club up sharply on the backswing, and chop steeply down on the ball.

Because you have the ball so far back in your stance, you are, in effect, delofting the club you use by many degrees. But don't be tempted to use the sand iron, because of the very great danger of bouncing the sole off the turf before meeting the ball. Do remember that, whichever club you choose, you will get a much lower flight trajectory, and so you can only use the lofted irons. Don't even think about using anything less than your 8-iron. If you do, you'll probably achieve no more than scuttling your ball along the ground.

When the ball is well below your feet, you must overcome a strong tendency to slice.

## BALL BELOW THE FEET

Here, the ball is also a good deal further away from you than normal. To get yourself nearer, you have to 'sit down to it' and also grip the club right at the end. As with all shots from severe slopes, you won't be able to make any real body turn, and particularly in this stance, that means a very strong tendency to slice. You can, however, aim off to allow for this left-to-right movement.

Your tendency to topple towards the ball must be resisted, but even an increased lean towards the ball increases the danger of shanking. Think, while you swing, that you mustn't bring this part of the club into the ball. Concentrate on bringing the centre of the club face into it.

# BALL ABOVE THE FEET

Here we have the reverse situation, but most players find it's an easier one to play, perhaps because the player is nearer to the ball. Anything which reduces the hand and eye co-ordination in a golf shot ought to make it easier.

This time, grip the club lower; when the ball is very much above your feet, you may even have to have the right hand off the grip and on the shaft. When you have to go this far, the question arises about what to do with the handle of the club.

There is a tendency for it to want to disappear into your stomach. The answer is to place your ball well forward in your stance, so that the handle now avoids your stomach, and projects beyond your left hip. It will still be in the way, but this is an awkward shot and you have to make the most of your possibilities to make a moderate – not a great – shot.

The tendency is to hook, although playing with the ball so far forward does reduce this danger. Again, allow for right-to-left movement of the ball by aiming off. You should get a low flight, and consequently, more run on dry ground.

In all these slope situations, we have been considering severe problems. Don't be over-ambitious: aim for a **result that gets you into a more favorable position.**

Grip the club lower when the ball is above your feet. Most players find this an easier shot to play than the opposite situation because they are nearer the ball.

# RESTRICTED BACKSWINGS

Wayward shots will often get you into situations where you can't swing back freely. If you're among trees, for example, a branch may impede the top of your swing. If you are really close up to a tree, you may have no room to swing at all.

Consider the alternatives. One option is to take a penalty drop. Another, is to play away from your target, aiming to get into a position where you have an open shot to the flag. You can also consider playing the shot left-handed, toe down. Yet another method is to play one-handed: this means turning your back on the target, and striking with the full face of the club.

Of these, only playing away from the target offers an easy shot. Most golfers don't practice them, but it's always possible to compensate for inexperience, to some extent, by rehearsing the shot a few times. You then carry out the shot you've rehearsed, and try to maintain your confidence. Above all do not change your shot in mid-swing, perhaps in an effort to force another 20 yards. The result is more likely to be stubbing the club into the ground, or even an air shot. You would have been far better off taking your medicine in the form of a penalty shot.

If you aren't playing through rough, don't forget your putter. It's the easiest club in the bag to use, especially one-handed, or with an unaccustomed grip.

So far, the discussion has been about extremely restricted backswings, or perhaps no space at all. It's far more usual, however, to get into situations where you have only to deal with limited restriction, as when your club would be impeded by a bush, or the lower branches of a tree.

Test out how severe the impediment is. Remember, you are not allowed to improve your position by repeatedly swinging into the obstruction, so you can't break twigs until the problem is eliminated. That costs penalty strokes.

You are, however, allowed to rehearse your stroke, just so long as you do not cause breakages. Quite frequently, you will be able to play a full stroke, when you find that there isn't anything of real substance in the way. Even so, it's all too easy to lose confidence at the last moment and make a badly timed shot.

On balance, it's better to take no chances. If you feel that your confidence isn't high enough, shorten the backswing so that you don't reach the obstruction, and rehearse your swing once again. Once more, do play the shot you've rehearsed. Don't be tempted, in an effort to gain just a few yards more, force your clubhead at the ball with a thrust of the hands. This will ruin the timing of the shot, and as likely as not, produce a total mis-hit.

The branches will restrict your backswing so rehearse your swing.

**OPPOSITE TOP LEFT:** Only a little jab is possible in this situation.

**OPPOSITE TOP RIGHT:** If the backswing is totally restricted you can only drop the ball under penalty. In the bottom picture, local rules may permit the drop without penalty.

**ABOVE AND OPPOSITE:** When playing awkward shots with obstructions in the way, practice the shot a couple of times first to find out how restricted you are in your swing and follow through. When you feel ready and have a mental picture of the shot in your mind, then play it.

# UNUSUAL SURFACES

On a golf course, you expect to be playing from grass. You won't often be disappointed, but there are exceptions. Let's think of an area of the Old Course at St Andrews, where there are two famous 'hazards' in the shape of roads.

One is called 'Grannie Clark's Wynd', a right of way, dating from time immemorial, crossing the first and last fairways, running from the town to the sea. A good shot from the tee at the par 4 1st hole will land well beyond it, but this isn't the case at the 18th. The other is the famous metalled track which gave the 17th its world-renowned name of 'The Road Hole'. It runs along the right of the fairway, and, then tight along the right-hand edge of the green.

If a good player's ball comes to rest on Grannie Clark's Wynd, he won't be much disturbed. He'll simply select his wedge or a 9-iron and pitch to the hole. The other road doesn't create much of a problem either. He can play off the road towards the flag, but may have great difficulty stopping his ball in time, if he tries to lob to the green. He can also roll the ball up the grassy slope between road and green, but will find it hard to get the right distance.

At club level, however, most golfers are quite bothered enough just at the thought of playing off a road surface, never mind finishing close to the flag.

**BELOW AND OPPOSITE:** The danger when playing off a road or gravel path is the possible damage to your club. However, shortening your hold should reduce the possibility of club damage.

So what should you do in this situation? First of all, study the local rules. You may find that you are allowed to drop off without penalty, and would choose to do so. You can also decide that a ball is unplayable, wherever you like, and drop off under penalty – that's if the local rules tell you that the road in question is part of the golf course.

Really though – this is just a little cowardly. As I've said, professionals facing this situation will play the ball as it lies with scarcely a pause for thought: the shot isn't really very difficult, though it does need precise striking.

Choose a club which will give you the right distance without forcing the shot, and grip it a little shorter. Swing smoothly, and you should get a good result. This is also important because of the very real danger of club damage. Swinging a club violently into contact with such an unforgiving surface could well mean a chip out of the leading edge of your iron, or the shaft may break off at the hosel. You can reduce your chances of this damage by not swinging full out – If your iron shots usually take a large divot after the ball, you will need a change of approach to avoid almost certain mayhem, and also prevent jarring of hands and wrists. The pro will try to nip the ball off the surface cleanly, knowing that he can rely on the loft of his club to give him backspin. You should do likewise, aiming to get the bottom of the blade under the ball, and then travelling along a line parallel with the hard surface, not into it. This way, you should clip the ground, not crack into it.

Before you play the shot off a difficult surface check the local rules, you may be entitled to a drop without penalty.

# GLOSSARY OF TECHNICAL TERMS USED

**Address**: standing to the ball, usually with the club grounded behind it.

**Advice**: a player may not ask, nor may he be told, how to play a shot of a hole. He may, however, ask and be given information. *See* 'information'.

**Arc**: the curve of the golf swing.

**Baffy**: a lofted wood with a short shaft, once used for pitching to greens.

**Balata**: a soft golf ball covering that in theory provides more adhesion between ball and clubface. This leads to greater backspin, but the balls become scuffed more easily.

**Blade**: the head of an iron club, sometimes including the putter when of similar shape to an iron.

**Borrow**: the slopes on a green that cause the ball to curve in the course of a putt.

**Carry**: the distance a ball travels in the air.

**Center-shaft**: a design of putter popular for many years. The essential feature is that the shaft is not fixed at the heel. Instead, it is fixed considerably nearer the center, so that the sweet spot is only a little towards the toe of the club in relation to where the shaft is joined to the clubhead.

**Chip**: a shot from near the green played towards the hole where the ball, for most of its travel, runs along the ground.

**Clearing the hips**: the counter-clockwise movement of the hips that allows the through swing to take place.

**Closed face**: position of the clubface in relation to the ball when the toe is slanted inwards;

also the position of the clubhead at the top of the backswing when the clubface is square to the target line instead of the toe pointing along it.

**Closed stance**: when the left foot is closer to the target line than the right.

**Cut**: a form of spin applied to the ball. It causes a left-to-right spin and shape of shot.

**Dogleg**: a shape of golf hole where, on a par 4 or par 5, the fairway bends sharply to the left or right.

**Draw**: a shape of golf shot where the ball starts traveling to the right of target and then curves gently right to left.

**Dying ball**: a ball still moving but coming close to the end of its travel.

**Embedded ball**: a ball that comes to rest in its own pitch mark.

**Equator**: an imaginary line running horizontally around the middle of a golf ball.

**Fade**: a shape of golf shot where the ball starts by traveling to the left of target and then curves gently left to right.

**Fairway woods**: wooden or, commonly, metal clubs with more loft than a driver. The most commonly used are the 3 and 4, but many golfers use a 2-wood and a 5-wood.

**Flange**: a body of metal added to the sole or rear of a club. In the case of a putter, the main purpose is to provide more weight.

**Flat putt**: a putt without borrow.

**Flat swing**: a swing in which the golfer's hands, arms, and club

are not above shoulder level in the backswing.

**Flex (of a shaft)**: bend.

**Follow-through**: the part of the golf swing that follows impact with the ball. Often applied to the end of the swing alone.

**Good turn**: when a golfer moves the shoulders 90 degrees or more on the backswing.

**Grain**: the direction of growth of grass on a green. When the growth is away from the player and along the line of putt, the ball will travel further for the same strength of strike – and vice versa.

**Green to play with**: a golfer has little green to play with when playing to a hole close to the edge of the green nearest to them. There is plenty of green to play with when the hole is considerably further away.

**Grip**: the action of holding a golf club.

**Ground under repair (GUR)**: parts of the golf course marked as unfit for play, from which a golfer can remove his ball without penalty.

**Hazard**: a bunker or marked area of water, stream, ditch, or river.

**Hickory**: the type of wood most frequently used for golf club shafts until steel was introduced in the late 1920s. Its use today is mainly confined to a limited number of putters. Hickory clubs are more difficult to use, for most, because the shaft is twisted as well as bent. By comparison, steel shafts have little such torque (twist).

**Hood**: to strike the ball with the hands ahead of the clubhead at the time of ball strike. Depending on the variation of this hand position, the loft is either slightly or considerably reduced.

**Hooded face:** the angle of a clubface when the golfer addresses or strikes the ball with the hands well ahead of the clubhead.

**Hook:** movement of the ball from right to left. The ball usually begins by traveling right of the target line and then begins curving left.

**Impact:** when clubhead strikes the ball.

**Information:** statements of fact on such topics as distances and direction. A strong distinction is made, under the Rules of Golf, between matters of fact (information) and advice.

**Interlocking:** a method of gripping where the little finger of the right hand and the forefinger of the left hand are entwined.

**Jerks:** the term has the same meaning as 'yips' and 'twitch'. All refer to an involuntary nervous movement, usually in the putting stroke but which can also occur in other short shots. This nervous movement is usually located in the hands, arms or wrists. Many great players have seen their careers come to an end as a result of this problem.

**Lateral head movement:** when the head moves backward, and perhaps forward, during the golf swing.

**Lateral movement (on the greens):** ball movements to either side.

**Lay up:** to play short (perhaps of some danger on the golf course).

**Leading edge:** the front rather than rear edge of a club.

**Lie:** how the ball is positioned on the ground.

**Loft:** the slope on the face of a golf club.

**Loop:** a golf swing when the clubhead does not travel back and down on merely the same path, but loops round in the top part of the backswing.

**Manipulating (with the hands):** consciously using the hands as a separate element in a golf swing.

**Mini-swing:** the golf swing in miniature.

**Open face:** position of the clubface in relation to the ball when the toe is slanted outwards; also the position of the clubhead at the top of the backswing, when the toe does not point along the target line but points away from the player to a greater or lesser extent.

**Open stance:** standing to the ball with left foot further away from the target line than the right.

**Out of bounds:** outside the boundaries of the golf course. These areas are usually around the perimeter of the course, but sometimes areas inside the perimeter are designated out of bounds – the practice ground is sometimes an example of this.

**Overlapping:** grip of the club in which the little finger of the right hand rests on, or just beyond, the forefinger of the left hand.

**Perimeter weighing:** a design concept found mainly in irons, but also in some putters and most metal woods, where much of the clubhead weight is concentrated around the clubhead rather than behind the center. The result is that an off-center strike will still be reasonably effective.

**Pitch:** a high shot, anywhere between 10 and 150 yards, when the ball travels mostly through the air and with relatively little run; also the point where a golf ball lands on the ground.

**Plane:** the arc followed by the clubhead through the golf swing. It may be 'in plane' or 'out of plane'.

**Pull hook:** a shot that goes to the left immediately from the clubface and then curves right to left.

**Punch:** manner of hitting a golf ball where the forearms dominate and there is less wrist movement than usual.

**Recovery shots:** these occur after a player has hit a shot into some difficulty. If the player can retrieve the situation completely they have 'recovered'. For example, if a player hits into a greenside bunker but putts their sand shot close to the hole, that is a recovery. If, however, they merely escape from that same bunker and not near to the hole, that is not a recovery.

**Relief:** times where you are permitted to move your ball and drop it elsewhere without penalty.

**Reverse overlap**: a grip used mostly in putting, but also in other short shots, where the left index finger is extended over the right hand.

**Royal and Ancient**: the golf club in St. Andrews, Scotland, much involved in administering aspects of the game of golf. One of its prime responsibilities is laying down the rules of golf in most countries. This it does in conjunction with the United States Golf Association, which bears this responsibility in North

America. The R and A, as it is often called in brief, also organizes the British Open Championship, and several other championships for amateurs. It also plays a role in the development of golf.

**Safe shot:** playing in a direction or to a length that avoids some danger, either on the fairway or the green, when a bolder shot would present both danger and the prospect of greater reward.

**Schenectady:** a mallet type putter with the shaft fixed towards the center of the clubhead. It was designed early this century and became very popular after the American Walter Travis won the British Amateur using one in 1904. Center-shaft putters were banned by the R and A a few years later (but not by the United States Golf Association) and the ban remained in force for almost fifty years. This was one of the main points that divided the two organizations as regards the rules of golf.

**Shaft:** all the golf club other than the head. Most often made of tubular steel with other materials, such as carbon fiber, aluminum, glass fiber, and wood.

**Shut face:** the position of the clubface in relation to the ball when the toe is slanted inwards; also the position of the clubhead at the top of the backswing when the toe of the club does not point along the target line but instead the clubface or clubhead is parallel with that line.

**Slice:** a shot where the ball immediately curves left to right from the clubface.

**Slot:** the position of the clubhead at the top of the backswing. Players aim to make this very consistent and may then say 'I'm getting the club in the slot' or 'I can't get the club in the slot.'

**Sole:** the part of a golf clubhead that rests on the ground when the ball is addressed.

**Square face:** when, at address, the clubface is parallel to an imaginary line drawn from ball to player.

**Square stance:** standing to the ball with both feet an equal distance from the target line.

**Stance:** position of the player as he or she stands to the ball, ready to swing.

**Straight-faced:** a club, usually said of an iron, when there is little loft on the clubface.

**Streak putter:** a player who putts brilliantly but only in relatively short spells, perhaps a few holes, a round of golf or even a whole tournament. A player who is not recognized as being a consistently good putter.

**Strong (wedge):** a club, usually but not always a wedge, with less loft than the norm, thus producing lower flight and more run.

**Sweet spot:** the small area on the putter face that gives the desired results when the ball is struck. The ball should then travel the anticipated distance. It will travel less far the further the strike is from the sweet spot.

**Swing path:** the route followed by the clubhead in backswing and downswing.

**Target line:** an imaginary line between ball and intended target.

**Tee:** an area of golf course from which players begin playing a particular hole.

**Tee peg:** a small device, usually made of wood, rubber, or plastic, on which golfers can place their ball before playing off from the teeing area.

**Tee shot:** a golf shot played from a teeing area.

**Tee-up:** to place a ball on a tee peg.

**Topspin:** where the ball rotates in flight, or from the clubhead, with top of the ball moving towards the bottom in a forward direction. Many consider this an impossibility in putting until the ball ceases to skid over the green and to begin rolling. However, a player can reduce the amount of backspin that naturally occurs by striking the center of the ball on the upswing and by using a putter with very little loft.

**Twitch:** *see* 'jerks'.

**Upright swing**: a swing where the player moves the club well above shoulder level, towards the head rather than the shoulder joint.

**Vardon grip:** *see* 'overlapping'.

**Waggle:** movements of the clubhead after the player has addressed the ball but before beginning to swing back and play their shot.

**Wedge:** a highly-lofted club used for short approach shots.

**Wrist-break:** bending or flexing of the wrist joint.

**Yardage chart:** any printed or handwritten product that shows distances from or to various points on a golf hole.

**Yips:** *see* 'jerks'.

# INDEX

Quantum Publishing would like to thank Ned Hoste for jacket design and Dorothy Frame for indexing.